CAI Modeling in Education

CAI Modeling in Education

A. R. Mohamed Ismail

SERIALS PUBLICATIONS
NEW DELHI (INDIA)

First Published - 2011

ISBN: 978-81-8387-452-6

Published by

SERIALS PUBLICATIONS
4830/24, Prahlad Street, Ansari Road
Darya Ganj, New Delhi-110002 (India)
Phone : 23245225 Fax : 91-11-23272135
E-mail: serials@sify.com

CONTENTS

ACKNOWLEDGEMENT

I am conscious of my indebtedness to each and every individual who helped me in many ways in the preparation of this thesis entitled *"Effect of CAI techniques on some selected cognitive and conative variables with respect to teaching of Double Integrals in Calculus at undergraduate level"*.

At the outset, let me thank the 'Almighty' for having bestowed His mercy on me to complete this research work.

I hereby acknowledge my gratitude to the honourable President, Secretary and Correspondent, Treasurer, Assistant Secretary and other members of the Management Committee of Jamal Mohamed College, and to our beloved Principal *Dr. M. Sheik Mohamed* for their encouragement and constant support in this endeavour. I also thank *Prof. N. Abdul Samadh* and *Dr. K. Abdullah Basha* former Principals for their encouragement.

I express my deep sense of gratitude to *Late Dr. V. Jayathilakan,* the Guide and Supervisor, for his valuable guidance and supervision all through the work.

My sincere thanks are due to *Major A. Balasubramanian,* Professor of Education, who initiated me to undergo this Ph.D work. Through him only, I have established contact with experts in the field of my research.

I express my sincere thanks to *Dr. P. S. Balasubramanian,* former Professor and Head, Department of Education, University of Madras for his valuable suggestions and help in this task. He has enriched me at every stage of my research work through his rich experience and enviable guidance.

I express my sincere thanks to *Dr. K. Ramanaiah, Dr. A.M. Mohamed Sindhasha, Dr. E. Mubarak Ali, Dr. M. Tajudeen,* and *Dr. Rasul Mohideen,* for their unstinted co-operation and valauble suggestions throughout the research work.

I extend my sincere thanks to *Late Dr. S. Purusothaman* and *Dr. R. Kanagaraj* for their help and co-operation at each and every stage of the progress of the thesis.

I express my gratitude to all my colleagues in the Department of Computer Science and Mathematics, both teaching and non-teaching for their kind help and encouragement in the completion of this research work.

My thanks are due to my teachers, colleagues, relations, friends and well wishers. It remains for me to express my thanks to my wife *Hajiah. M.I. Kurshidh Begum,* my son *Er. M.I. Mohamed Khaleelur Rahman* and my daughters *M.I. Sadhuna Parveen Banu and M.I. Thahira Thasneen and my in-laws* for their assistance and encouragement all throughout.

I record my thanks to the students of Bachelor of Science, Jamal Mohamed College who have responded to my request and participated in this experiment.

I express my sincere thanks to the publisher, Serials Publications, New Delhi-2 who accepted to bring my research study into a book form.

A. R. Mohamed Ismail

CHAPTER 1

THE STUDY

INTRODUCTION

This is the age of computers. The introduction of computers has revolutionized our life. The widespread application is seen in every field of activity whether science, education, industry, commerce or war. Computer has been accepted as an indispensable extension of human intellect in the scientific and business world. In education too, the computer is fast becoming an indispensable tool to amplify the learner's capabilities. It will enhance the educational productivity in teaching students to be creative, to think critically, to make valid decisions and to explain and present their ideas in a precise manner. It is needless to say that computers cannot replace teachers. The teachers would continue to play a vital role in the learning process of the students using microcomputers specially as a teaching aid. In this context this experimental study has been undertaken with a view to studying the effect of *CAI* (Computer Assisted Instruction) techniques on some selected cognitive and conative variables with respect to the teaching of 'Double Integrals' in Calculus at the undergraduate level.

IMPORTANCE OF THE STUDY

Microcomputers presently have a tremendous influence on teaching of subjects like mathematics in schools and colleges.

It has become an essential machine not only for business but also for classrooms. They are being used as resources in teaching and learning at all levels of education and training. This process is known as CAL – Computer Assisted Learning. Learners can sit in front of terminals and communicate directly with a computer in a conversational mode. Using this mode, a learner can learn a topic at his own time and pace. Computers are also used to manage the learning process. This is called Computer Managed Learning (CML). Computers can store a student responses, evaluate his performance and then direct him to the next learning unit.

It is obvious that computers may also assist in instructional programme. The computer has several distinct advantages over other conventional instruction media. These include its almost unlimited storage capacity (memory), its accurate and rapid retrieval of information, its problem-solving capacities, and its versatility in terms of possible modes of presentation. In addition, it is also claimed that of all instructional media, computer is the only one medium that communicates on a completely individualized basis. It gives modified responses depending upon the person using it. Computers are being used for teaching of mathematics like any other subject.

There is no dispute regarding the need for teaching mathematics as a part of general education in every society. Teaching Mathematics has moved from a subject oriented to learner centered activity and finally to society centered approach.

Mathematics is a subject that demands regularity. If a student is absent even for a few days, the sequence is broken and he fails to comprehend the subsequent steps. Nervous and rash students are also not likely to do well in this subject. Moreover, this subject demands full concentration which some students may not be able to give. Only when a proper approach in its teaching is adopted, the really intelligent students will come to the forefront. Only high achievers will survive and weak students will not flourish. To remove their nervousness and confusion, the teacher should try to develop self-confidence in the students. It is therefore, necessary to inculcate the habit of learning by self effort of learners. Computers come to our help in this regard.

The introduction of computers in mathematics teaching at the college level is still in its infant stage. Though some software programmes were prepared, they were meant only for demonstration purposes and students cannot do their experiments on their own. The most important reason for dullness in *CAI* is paucity of teachers trained in the use of computers for mathematical education. The software prepared by the professionals normally does not suit the local needs. Therefore, attention has been drawn to the development, application and evaluation of Computer Assisted Instructions in the teaching of mathematics.

STATEMENT OF THE PROBLEM

Mathematics as a discipline has several sub branches and calculus is one such branch. Integral calculus, as part of the concept of calculus, consists of integrals involving one or more variables. Double integrals is a difficult concept to grasp and understand from the learner's viewpoint. This is a concept which is taught at the undergraduate level for the first year degree students who study mathematics either as a major subject or as an allied subject. When the Double Integrals concept is taught through the traditional chalk and talk method of teaching, generally the learners find it difficult to understand this concept. This is because, there is no possibility for visualizing the movements of areas and volumes through finite strips which are essential for understanding the concept of Double Integrals. This is not possible in any of the conventional methods of Instruction. However, this is quite possible when this concept is taught through *CAI*. The researcher has developed a software package which will enable the learners to learn, grasp and understand the concept of Double Integrals without any difficulty. Further, the investigator has also made an attempt to study the effect of *CAI* package developed with respect to the teaching and learning of Double Integrals in calculus at the undergraduate level.

RATIONALE FOR SELECTION OF THE TOPIC

The natural interest in the subjects viz., Mathematics and Computer Science has enthused the researcher to choose this topic relating to teaching and learning of Mathematics through Computer Assisted Instruction. The investigator being a teacher in Mathematics and Computer Science with Post-graduate degrees and diploma in Mathematics, Educational technology and Computer Science has evinced a keen interest in the present study and research.

The researcher has consulted Professors of mathematics, computer science and educational psychology with rich experience and qualified software programmers before the selection of this topic. Most of the subject experts expressed the view that 'Double Integration' from the principle of Riemann sum is comparatively abstract and difficult concept to comprehend in Mathematics. Further, Computer Assisted Instruction for teaching and learning 'Double Integrals' would benefit thousands of students studying Mathematics as a major or as an allied subject to understand the concept early. This prompted the researcher to choose this topic of study.

OBJECTIVES OF THE STUDY

The following objectives were framed for the study:

1. To develop and validate a *CAI* package on 'Double Integrals' for undergraduate students.
2. To determine the preferential index of the students i.e., their choice between Computer Assisted Instruction and conventional method of instruction.
3. To compare the achievement of the learners taught through *CAI* and conventional method of instruction in 'Double Integrals'.
4. To find out the achievement of the learners taught through *CAI* and conventional method of instruction in 'Double Integrals' for selected cognitive and conative variables viz., knowledge, understanding, application and skill.

5. To understand the impact of the select variables, viz., sex, medium of instruction and locale of the learners, on their achievement when they learn through *CAI.*
6. To know the influence of the variables viz., sex, medium of instruction and locale on the achievement of the learners based on knowledge, understanding, application and skill.
7. To find out the relationship between the variables such as Family income, Educational status of father, Educational status of mother, Size of the family and the achievement of undergraduate students when they learn 'Double Integrals' through *CAI.*
8. To find out the contribution of the factors such as Family income, Educational status of father, Educational status of mother, Size of the family to the achievement of undergraduate students in 'Double Integrals' when they learn through *CAI* at different selected cognitive and conative variables viz., knowledge, understanding, application and skill.
9. To identify the most dominant factor which influences the achievement of the learners who learn 'Double Integrals' through *CAI.*
10. To find out the most important factor, which influences the achievement of the learners, based on knowledge, understanding, application and skill.

SCOPE OF THE STUDY

The present study is an attempt to introduce *CAI* as the learning strategy for the concept of 'Double Integrals', where more attention is paid to concretise the abstract ideas through animations and development of problem solving exercises using Mathmatics programming propagated by Gilbert, an eminent psychologist, to enable self-learning by the students.

The study was confined to the first year undergraduate students studying Mathematics either as a major or as an allied subject, as the concept of 'Double Integrals' is part of their curriculum. The conventional method of instruction on 'Double

Integrals' was carried out for 15 hours for each group of the total number of sample students spread over a period of 3 months from August 2001 to October 2001. During the same period, the experimental group of students were exposed to the self-learning process of *CAI* in the same topic.

HYPOTHESES

The following hypotheses were formulated on the basis of the objectives framed:

1. Undergraduate students who were taught 'Double Integrals' through *CAI* and conventional instruction methods differ significantly in their post-test achievement scores.
2. Undergraduate students learning 'Double Integrals' through *CAI* and conventional instruction methods differ significantly in their achievement.
3. Undergraduate students with rural background, learning 'Double Integrals' through *CAI* and conventional instruction methods differ significantly in their achievement.
4. Undergraduate students with urban background learning 'Double Integrals' through *CAI* and conventional instruction methods differ significantly in their achievement.
5. Undergraduate male students, learning 'Double Integrals' through *CAI* and conventional instruction methods differ significantly in their achievement.
6. Undergraduate female students, learning 'Double Integrals' through *CAI* and conventional instruction methods differ significantly in their achievement.
7. Undergraduate students, who studied in Tamil medium (at their secondary school level), learning 'Double Integrals' through *CAI* and through conventional instruction methods differ in their achievement.
8. Undergraduate students, who were taught in English (at their secondary school level), learning 'Double

Integrals' through *CAI* and conventional instruction methods differ in their achievement.

9. In learning 'Double Integrals' through *CAI* at undergraduate level, students with rural background differ significantly from the students with urban background in their achievement.
10. In learning 'Double Integrals' through *CAI* at undergraduate level, male students differ significantly from female students in their achievement.
11. In learning 'Double Integrals' through *CAI* at undergraduate level, students studied in Tamil medium and English medium at secondary school level differ significantly in their achievement.
12. Undergraduate students learning 'Double Integrals' through *CAI* and conventional instruction methods differ significantly in their
    - (i) Knowledge
    - (ii) Understanding
    - (iii) Application
    - (iv) Skill
13. Undergraduate students with rural background learning 'Double Integrals' through *CAI* and conventional instruction methods differ significantly in their
    - (i) Knowledge
    - (ii) Understanding
    - (iii) Application
    - (iv) Skill
14. Undergraduate students with urban background learning 'Double Integrals' through *CAI* and conventional instruction methods differ significantly in their
    - (i) Knowledge
    - (ii) Understanding

(iii) Application
(iv) Skill

15. Undergraduate male students, learning 'Double Integrals' through *CAI* and conventional instruction methods differ significantly in their
    (i) Knowledge
    (ii) Understanding
    (iii) Application
    (iv) Skill
16. Undergraduate female students learning 'Double Integrals' through *CAI* and conventional instruction methods differ significantly in their
    (i) Knowledge
    (ii) Understanding
    (iii) Application
    (iv) Skill
17. Undergraduate students, who studied in Tamil medium (at their secondary school level), learning 'Double Integrals' through *CAI* and conventional instruction methods differ in their
    (i) Knowledge
    (ii) Understanding
    (iii) Application
    (iv) Skill
18. Undergraduate students, who studied in English medium (at their secondary school level), learning 'Double Integrals' through *CAI* and conventional instruction methods differ in their
    (i) Knowledge
    (ii) Understanding
    (iii) Application
    (iv) Skill

19. In learning 'Double Integrals' through *CAI* at undergraduate level students with rural background differ significantly from the students with urban background in their.
    (i) Knowledge
    (ii) Understanding
    (iii) Application
    (iv) Skill
20. In learning 'Double Integrals' through *CAI* at undergraduate level, male students differ significantly from female students in their
    (i) Knowledge
    (ii) Understanding
    (iii) Application
    (iv) Skill
21. In learning 'Double Integrals' through *CAI* at undergraduate level, students who studied in Tamil medium differ significantly from the students who studied in English medium (at their secondary school level) in their
    (i) Knowledge
    (ii) Understanding
    (iii) Application
    (iv) Skill
22. Parental education influences the achievement of the learners, when they learn 'Double Integrals' through *CAI*.
23. Parental education influences the achievement of the learners based on knowledge, understanding, application and skill, when they learn 'Double Integrals' through *CAI*.

OPERATIONAL DEFINITIONS

The problem of the present study is stated as "Effect of *CAI* techniques on some selected cognitive and conative variables with respect to teaching of Double Integrals in Calculus at undergraduate level".

The key terms used in this research work have been operationally defined as follows:

Effect

Oxfort Advanced Learner's Dictionary defines the word 'effect' as an exchange produced by an action or a cause; a result or an outcome. In this study the word refers to the scholastic achievement produced by Computer Assisted Instruction as its outcome.

CAI

CAI (Computer Assisted Instruction) in this study refers to 'A mode of teaching with the help of computer'. It implies the self-learning process to acquire knowledge and understanding and also to develop application and skill.

Cognitive and Conative Variables

Cognitive and Conative variables in this study refer to the selected four variables viz., knowledge, understanding, application and skill. These behavioural variables are the outcome of Benjamin Blooms's 'Taxonomy of Educational objectives'. 'Cognitive' is an adjective to the word 'cognition' which means the action or process of acquiring knowledge and understanding and its application. Conative refers to the development of skill.

Double Integrals

Double Integral is the integral of a function of two variables as the limit of a sum. In other words, the succession of integrals in which integration is to be performed first with respect to one variable, the second being held constant, then with respect to the other variable.

According to Riemann – Stieltjes, the 'Double Integral' is defined as follows :

Suppose $f(x,y)$ is continuous and bounded on

$$R = \{ (x,y) \ / \ a \le x \le b, c \le y \le d \}$$

Then the double integral of $f(x,y)$ over R is defined as,

$$\iint_R f(x,y)\, dA = \lim_{m,n \to \infty} \sum_{i=1}^{m} \sum_{j=1}^{n} f(x_{ij}^*, y_{ij}^*)\, \Delta A$$

where $(x_{ij}^*, y_{ij}^*) \in R_{ij} = \{ (x,y) / x_{i-1} \leq x < x_i, y_{j-1} \leq y \leq y_j \}$

and ΔA is the area of R_{ij}

EXPERIMENTAL DESIGN

Since the primary objective of this study is to find out the effect of *CAI* on learning 'Double Integrals' by the undergraduate students, the experimental method has to be adopted by the investigator.

To study the effect of teaching through *CAI* as compared to the conventional method, the investigator adopted the 'Two group Experimental Design' where the two groups were treated with two different instructional techniques assigned at random. Conventional method of instruction was followed to the students in the control group. *CAI* is to be used for experimental group.

The Pre-test and Post-test Experimental Design was followed for this study.

The sample is proposed to divided into two different groups viz., the Experimental group and the Control group. The Control group was taught allowed to learn through conventional methods of teaching whereas the experimental group was exposed to *CAI* techniques. At the end of the experiment, the difference between the mean scores of Control group and the Experimental group in the achievement of 'Double Integral was analysed statistically'

LIMITATIONS OF THE STUDY

This study is not without limitations. They are:

1. This study is limited to the first year undergraduate students who selected Mathematics either as a major or as an allied subject.
2. This study is limited to the certain concepts of 'Double integrals' only.

3. This study is limited to the selected sample from a selected college only ie, 282 students from Jamal Mohamed College, Tiruchirappalli, Tamil Nadu.
4. Only the selected cognitive and conative variables were taken into consideration for analyzing the scholastic achievement of the students.

CHAPTERIZATION

Chapter 1 - The study

Chapter 2 - *CAI* – Conceptual Framework

Chapter 3 - Review of Related Literature

Chapter 4 - Research Procedure

Chapter 5 - Effect of *CAI* in teaching and learning 'Double Integrals'-An Analysis

Chapter 6 - Findings and Suggestions.

CHAPTER 2

CAI – CONCEPTUAL FRAMEWORK

MATHEMATICS AND TEACHING OF MATHEMATICS

The history of human civilization reveals the necessity of counting, measuring, weighing and drawing in all aspects of environment. Quantitative sciences soon gained phenomenal advancement. Mathematics is an integral part of the universe whose every aspect is quantitative. In every profession connected with applied sciences, a working knowledge of mathematical concept is a necessity to understand the deep foundations which carry the various subjects upon them. It is therefore, a strong base of mathematics education is considered to be an absolute necessity for all.

In the fast progressing world, most of the students find what is being done in the classroom is dull, uninteresting and irrelevant, the learning culture has changed but not the teaching culture. Education can be interactional in addition to being instructional. In this context, no one can deny the role of computer in the field of education.

Research in this area is new in its dimension and it has slowly attracted researchers in the developing countries. The main aim of education is to achieve a behavioral change and whether that could be brought about through computer is a big question. This research tries to find out an answer in this regard. A study of this kind requires a brief understanding of mathematics, its teaching and the application of computer in the teaching of mathematics.

Mathematics

According to various definitions, mathematics is the science of measurement, quality and magnitude. According to New English Dictionary, "Mathematics, in a strict sense, is the abstract science which investigates deductively the conclusions implicit in the elementary conceptions of spatial and numerical relations". It has also been defined as the science of number and space. The Sanskrit word for it is "Ganita" which means the science of calculation. It is a systematized, organized and exact branch of science. Mathematics is a way to settle in the mind a habit of reasoning.

Mathematics in Everyday Life

The knowledge of mathematics was developed out of the felt needs of human beings. Right from human existence on this earth, mathematics has been a faithful companion. Man invented arithmetic to answer the questions: How many ? How much? How long? How far? How big ? etc. Algebra was devised to simplify arithmetical computations. For measurement and form, geometry was invented. To find the position of high mountains and stars, trigonometry was invented and developed and so on in the case of numerous other branches of mathematics.

There is a definite need for mathematics in everybody's life for a long term planning and day-to-day planning. A human being is always for profitable and increasing returns. A mathematical approach is essential for any progress.

Even the most ordinary citizen has got to calculate his wages and buy things from bazaar. A person may be a mere housewife, farmer or labourer etc., but some knowledge of mathematics is absolutely necessary for any one. The entire atmosphere is surcharged with mathematics. The prices, rates, discounts, commissions, rebates, interests, taxes, shortages, production, distribution, inflation etc. are the issues with which everybody is intimately concerned. All the illustrations and arguments in favour of practical value of mathematics can be utilized and repeated to justify the place of the subject in day-to-day life.

Teaching of Mathematics

The present philosophy of mathematics education aims at a five dimensional role for the subject. The students learn it in the following ways:

(a) Functional use

(b) A subject of study

(c) An optional

(d) A discipline for specialization

(e) Research.

The outcome is that the student acquires the culture of the subject so that he or she reads mathematics, uses mathematics and creates mathematics. A good mathematics education should be a happy blending of learning mathematics rigoursly and also acquiring skills to solve problems.

The scientific approach to the pedagogy has laid down the following objectives in mathematics education:

(a) To develop in the pupil, the habits of logical thinking, inquisitiveness of mind and modelling ability.

(b) To equip them with the knowledge of fundamentals of mathematics and some skills.

(c) To make them learn to apply mathematics in science, technology, industry, agriculture, business and in day-to-day life.

These objectives of mathematics education are more relevant in the teaching and learning of mathematics at the higher level in the colleges and universities. Mathematics education serves the following purposes:

(a) To enable the pupils to solve mathematical problems of daily life.

(b) To develop in the pupil an acquaintance with his culture.

(c) To provide a suitable type of discipline in the minds of the learners.

(d) To prepare the pupil for technical professions such as those of accountants, auditors, bankers, surveyors, cashiers, engineers, scientists, statisticians and teachers.

(e) To prepare the pupil for economic, purposeful, productive, creative and constructive living.

(f) To develop the habits of concentration, self-reliance and discovery.

(g) To create in the pupils love for hard work.

(h) To develop in the pupils the powers of logical thinking and reasoning.

(i) To develop in him/her a scientific and realistic attitude towards life.

(j) To ensure in them accuracy and efficiency in fundamental processes and develop appreciation for accuracy.

The Present Scenario of Mathematics Teaching

Mathematics has been a peculiar subject. There is no dispute regarding the need for teaching mathematics as a part of general education in every society. Mathematics education has moved from a subject oriented to child centred to society centred approach during the present century.

Still, mathematics has been often ignored and more often disliked by many parents, pupils and teachers. Surveys continue to show that it is regarded as most difficult and unpleasant subject by majority of school children. (Sarasa, 1992).

Singh and Siddhu refer to a probe conducted in America to find out the causes of inefficiency of higher technological institutions, in which the "inefficiency was traced to, or attributed to, deteriorating standards of teaching in mathematics".

It should be frankly admitted that the present day teaching of mathematics is far from being satisfactory. The rate of failure in the subject is considerably higher than that of other subjects. This is not due to the drawbacks of any single agency at work.

Everybody has a complaint against the teaching of mathematics. It is dull, boring and difficult from the point of view of the learner. The teacher clings to traditional methods, because these offer the path of least resistance. The powers of thinking, understanding and retention are not thus developed in the students. There is no emphasis on thought, understanding, initiative, judicious study and power.

Therefore, the present state of teaching mathematics in the majority of educational institutions at all levels needs a lot of overhauling. There are different types of reforms required in teaching of mathematics. It is the joint responsibility of all concerned to bring about necessary improvements and changes. The remedy necessitates a fundamental change in values. Intelligent understanding should be the teacher's guiding principle. The teacher should not talk too much. He should teach and not preach mathematics. Computer can lend a helping hand in this regard.

COMPUTERS

Of all the 'explosions', we have heard in recent years, one of the most exciting is the 'knowledge explosion'. The world has learnt more about science and technology in the last three or four decades. Every advancement in the society in these days is influenced by computers. This is the age of computers. The introduction of computers has revolutionised the mode of our life. It's application is wide spread in every field of activity whether scientific, education, industry, commerce or defence. Computer has been accepted as an indispensable extension of human intellect in the scientific and business world. In education too, computer is fast becoming an important 'tool' in amplifying the knowledge and capabilities of the learners. It is to be stressed here that computers cannot replace teachers. The teacher would play a pivotal role in the learning process of the students and the computers are used specially as a teaching aid.

Definition of Computer

Computer can be defined as an electronic data processing machine which receives and stores any amount of information in the form of symbols and digits and process them at a tremendous speed as per the instructions and outputs the results with a desired degree of accuracy. In short, it is an electronic device for storing and analyzing information fed into it, for calculating or controlling machinery automatically.

Evolution of Computers

Computer's history starts with the development of a device called ABACUS by the Chinese around 300 B.C. Abacus consists of a wooden frame in which beads are threaded on wires. There are about 10 wires strung parallel on the frame. Abacus is being still used in the nursery schools for teaching basic arithmetic operations by sliding beads on wires.

The first computer developed was in the form of a mechanical calculating machine in 1642 by French mathematician, Blaise Pascal. In 1823, Charles Babbage, an Englishman made, "Difference Engine", which was able to evaluate algebraic expressions. Babbage also designed an automatic arithmetic machine, called 'Analytical Engine' in 1833. This design did not materialize for want of suitable fabrication technology at that time. The modern computers work on the same principle of analytical engine.

Dr. Herman Hollerith, an American, made an improved type of mechanical computer in 1890 which used punched cards as a media to feed information to the computer. The principle of representing symbols by punching holes on the cards was first designed by Hollerith. This method of coding is still in use in the modern digital computers.

The first electronic computer was ENIAC (Electronic Numerical Integrator and Calculator) had a formal dedication ceremony on 15th February, 1946. The next important development was the UNIVAC in 1951. UNIVAC was the beginning of the first generation of computers.

Man has invented many electronic devices but the computer has made a greater impact on society than any other single device. They have made significant contribution to the society during the last three decades.

The spate of innovations and inventions during the last decade has led to the development of mini, micro and personal computers. They are so versatile that they have become indispensable to engineers, scientists, businessmen, executives, managers, administrators, and others.

Modern computers possess certain characteristics and abilities that are peculiar to them. They can

(a) perform complex and repetitive calculations rapidly and accurately.

(b) store large amount of data and information for subsequent manipulation.

(c) hold a program of a model which can be explored in many different ways.

(d) make decisions.

(e) provide information to the user.

(f) automatically correct or modify - by providing signals- certain parameters of a system under control.

(g) draw and print graphs.

(h) converse with users through terminals.

Computers in Different Fields

Engineers and Scientists make use of the high speed computing capability of computers to solve their complex research and design problems.

Computers are used extensively in manufacturing and processing industries, power distribution systems, airline reservation systems, transportation systems and so on. Computer Aided Design (CAD) and Computer Aided Manufacturing (CAM) are becoming popular among the large industrial establishments.

Modeling and Simulation are other areas where computers are increasingly used. This has greatly accelerated research in such areas as physical sciences, medicine, astronomy and social science.

Business and commercial organizations need to store and maintain voluminous records and use them for various purposes such as inventory control, sales analysis, pay-roll accounting, resources scheduling and management reports. Computers can store and maintain the files and can sort, merge and update them whenever necessary.

The ability of computers to store large amount of data has led to their application in libraries, documentation - offices (centers), employment exchanges, police department, hospital and similar establishments. Computers are used in international games such as the Olympics and the Asiad to keep track of events and provide timely and reliable information and documentation to all concerned.

COMPUTERS IN EDUCATION

Computers are being used as resources in teaching and learning at all levels of education and training. This process is known as Computer Assisted Learning. Learners can sit at terminals and communicate directly with a computer in a conversational mode. Using this mode, a learner can learn a topic at his own time and pace.

Computers are also used to manage the learning process. This is called Computer Managed Learning (CML). Computers can store student responses, evaluate his performance and then direct him to the next learning unit.

The "Information Revolution" now very much in the offing seems to have a major impact on humanity. Computers have revolutionized communication. One can expect communication to become integrated with classroom computing in the same way, it is happening in every administrative network. Science and technology have become inseparable. Computer Aided Instruction and teaching are of vital importance in the modern setting. It has become common for authors to include a software "diskette" in the back cover of their books published for the learners to use while reading or learning their text.

In short, computers can be used in an educational environment in three ways:

(a) To instruct learners

(b) To assist teachers and

(c) To help in managing the institution

The first two uses are of our interest where the computer is used as a potential tool to aid the teaching – learning process. It becomes an effective instructional tool in the hands of an efficient teacher.

As an instructional tool it can play various roles effectively. However, the teacher and the learner are concerned with two significant roles only.

(a) Deliver instructions directly to students by allowing them to interact with the learning materials already programmed into the system.

(b) Manage information about learner performance and learning resource options in order to prescribe and control individualized lessons.

First role refers to Computer Assisted Learning (CAL) or Computer Assisted Instruction (*CAI*) and second role refers to Computer Managed Learning (CML) or Computer Managed Instruction (CMI). A Computer can be viewed as a tool for enhancing instruction and instructional management through Computer Assisted Instruction and Computer Managed Instruction respectively. Compared to Computer Assisted Instruction, the Computer Managed Instruction is still in its infancy in the developing countries.

COMPUTER ASSISTED INSTRUCTION (*CAI*)

CAI is the natural outgrowth of the application of the principles of programmed learning. It is an instructional technique in which the computer is used in the following ways:

(a) To control the presentation of stimuli to the learners.

(b) To accept and evaluate the learners' responses, and

(c) To present further stimuli based on those responses.

The learner uses a terminal directed by a computer that may be in the same room or some distance away. The terminal is generally equipped with information display and the learner response devices. The most common information display device is the Visual Display unit which looks like a TV screen. The most common learner response device is the key board which has keys similar to those in the typewriter. Computer Assisted Learning is concerned with the use of computers to mediate in the flow of information in the learning process. There may be, flows between the learner and the factual information that he or she must absorb, feedback to the learner on his or her progress, information about a model with which the learner is working, or flows between the learner and his or her teacher. This provides a framework for looking at *CAI* in more detail, for several different methods and modes of *CAI* can be identified by considering the way in which the computer is used to mediate the information flows.

Within this medium of *CAI*, there are a number of modes, which in practice overlap and are often used in combination. Since the field of computer in education is so recent, it is sometimes difficult to set up categories of modes. Distinctions between categories changes as new uses for computers are implemented. The following classification is generally accepted by the educationists.

(i) Tutorial
(ii) Drill and Practice
(iii) Simulation and Gaming
(iv) Problem - solving
(v) Computer based testing
vi) Browsing.

Tutorial

Tutorial programmes present information to the learner, usually by setting up a dialogue with the learner by asking questions. The question may be asked to give an option or to test the understanding of the learner. Depending on the learner's response, the computer might go to new material, repeat the information or branch to less difficult material. Generally, when the learner gives a wrong answer, the computer presents remedial teaching helping the learner to understand what is wrong in learner's response. The remedial teaching might consist of presenting the material in simpler steps. In its simplest form, this tutorial dialogue bears a close resemblance to the programmed learning sequences found in print and on teaching machines in the 1960's. It is reasonable to ask what computer can add to the material apart from illuminating the text. If that were all, then there could be little benefit in using the computer, a book would be better. However, programmed texts present a number of problems, particularly in determining whether the student has really mastered the current step and in deciding how to branch to the new step. Self–assessment in programmed texts may require the student to make difficult judgments and the routing may involve complex decisions based on the learner's performance. This responsibility may make the students work more, rather than less difficult.

To overcome this problem, computer can be used not only to present the learning information but also to determine the student's needs and preferences, and to decide how to branch through the structured material. Thus, the material can be made more complex without adding to the students burden and the assessment of the learners becomes objective.

Drill and Practice

In this type of program, no new material is presented. Instead, facts, ideas or relationships are practiced by giving a question or other appropriate stimulus to which the user must respond. The program will then tell the user whether the response is right or wrong, perhaps giving a hint and another try, before going to the next question.

Drill and practice programs vary greatly in their levels of sophistication, ranging from the unimaginative electronic ditto sheet to elaborate and exciting video games. This type of programs are widely used in science teaching and language learning. The untiring patience of the computer is utilised in this type of programs to enable the learners to reach the mastery level.

Simulation and Gaming

In simulation, the learner confronts a scale-down approximation or simplification or an abstraction of a real-life situation. The simulation program on flying plane gives the user experience in many aspects of flying a plane without any risk. In simulations, participants usually play a role that involves them in interactions with elements of the simulated environment. For example, the computer based simulation operation 'Frog' allows a student to dissect and reconstruct a frog using the same 'instruments' that would be used in a biology laboratory. The student must remove the twenty three organs in sequence as in an actual dissection. A large number of civilian and military occupations involve the operation or maintenance of complex equipment such as aircraft, manufacturing machines, weapon systems, nuclear power plants and oil rigs. Major airlines and the military use computer based simulators to reduce the amount of actual flying time required for training. The navy has reduced pilot training costs through the use of computer based simulation.

Computer has added a new dimension to game playing. In the days earlier to computer, games generally required two or more people. After the invention of the computers, it is now possible for an 'individual' to play a game against the computer. Since, most children find games to be a good motivation, computerized educational games may be used to motivate even the most reluctant learner to learn new concepts, practice previously learned skills or take tests.

Problem-Solving

Problem-solving programs fall into two categories, those the learner himself writes and those written by some one else to help the learner in solving problems. In learner-written programs, the learner defines a problem logically and writes a computer program to solve it. The computer will do the necessary calculations and or manipulations to provide the answers. In the second category, the computer is the problem solver. The computer makes the calculations while the student manipulates the variables. In the second category the computer plays the role of a sophisticated calculator.

Computer-based Testing

Computer can be used to store and file banks of test items. The test items can be filed by subject content, objectives measured, and or level of difficulty. Items in the bank can be rapidly updated and modified, new items added, and old items deleted with minimal effort. From the pool of test items the instructor can choose the items to include on an examination, or the computer can be programmed to select the items, either randomly or according to specified parameters.

Browsing

The last of the six major modes of *CAI* uses the computer as a mentor and guide through a range of learning resources which might, but need not be themselves based on a computer. The power of the computer to store, retrieve, and process information is used to help the student as he or she browses through the material, responding to questions about related information, retrieving items which are needed, summarizing statistical data, and suggesting possible lines of investigation that may be of interest.

The six modes of *CAI* discussed above need not be treated as water-tight compartments. They can be used in a variety of combinations to form the basis for newer outcomes. This gives *CAI* the ability to match specific learning problems by overcoming the weaknesses in one by the strengths of another. For example, simulations may be supported by some tutorial material and calculation facilities may be found in packages which are predominantly used in drill and practice. Most of the successful *CAI* programs in the software market are found to be combinations of the different modes of *CAI*.

CAI AS A LEARNING MEDIUM

The main strength of the computer as a learning medium is its ability to process information very quickly and accurately. The set of rules – the computer program which specifies the way in which the formation is to be manipulated – can be very complex, yet the processing can be completed so quickly as to appear almost instantaneous to the learner. This makes it possible for the computer to accept and act upon a variety of different kinds of response from the learner and to provide information in textual, graphical and animated form. Computer can control and co-ordinate information from other equipments like a slide projector or videodisc player and based on the learner's progress through a piece of structured material. It can make sophisticated decisions as to what course to follow next. This gives it an ability to respond to the learner's needs, difficulties and progress which is very much greater than that of a book or video.

The interactive nature of Computer Assisted Instruction, allows students to learn at their own pace. It helps to elicit high speed personalized responses and to get personalized instruction response. It also enables to receive feedback removing the social stigma of learning slowly or making errors and to maintain the record keeping ability with time saving.

The above mentioned attributes of *CAI* as a learning medium reveal that application of computers in education is a process of endless experimentation where one discovers how enormous the potentials are in terms of content, technique and flexibility. It is in the hands of those involved in the system of education - teachers, learners and educational administrators to make the best use of it. Since human resource development is one of the vital areas of current research, it is necessary to explore the possibilities of computer utilization for optimum development of human resources.

COMPUTER IN MATHEMATICS EDUCATION

The computer revolution has a far-reaching influence on mathematics education. Modern computers possess certain characteristics and abilities that are peculiar to them. They perform complex and repetitive calculations rapidly and accurately; store large amount of data and information for subsequent manipulation, hold a program of a model which can be explored in many different ways; make decisions; provide information to the user; automatically collect or modify - by providing signals - certain parameters of a system under control; draw and print graphs; converse with users through terminals.

These characteristics make computer a great boon to mathematics education in the following ways:

(a) The use of computers can save at least 25% of a student's time spent in routine calculations which are all monotonous and dull and are the most uninteresting and distasteful part of mathematics.

(b) The dislike of mathematic arises because of the anxiety over the mistakes that the students usually commit in these calculations, which the computers can do accurately in no time at all.

(c) The time saved can be used for giving students deeper insight into established and modern mathematical concepts.

(d) The time saved can also be used for giving the students training in mathematical modeling and a first-hand experience of the great powers of application of mathematics.

(e) The students can do a great deal of experimentation with numbers; can discover patterns in mathematics; can make conjunctures; can get a training in the process of mathematics.

(f) By finding counter-examples to conjectures, they can be convinced of the need for proofs in mathematics.

(g) The true impact of discovery approach, pattern recognition approach and freedom in learning can be realized fully by the use of computers.

CAI IN LEARNING DOUBLE INTEGRALS

In Mathematics most of the concepts of Integral calculus including 'Double Integrals' are found to be abstract. The abstract concepts can be explained easily through 2D and 3D figures using computers with animation techniques. Geometrical meaning and interpretation can be registered in the minds of the students very lucidly through these techniques. In addition to that the abstract ideas of 'Double

Integrals' can be made clear and concrete. With the help of computers, drill and practice can be provided to the students effectively. The programmed learning techniques can also be implemented without any difficulty through *CAI*. Thus, researcher has proposed to developed an interactive software package on learning 'Double Integrals'.

Programmed Instruction

Pragrammed instruction is a systematically planned, empirically established and effectively controlled self-instructional technique for providing individualized instruction to the learner through logically sequenced small segments of the subject matter by using the principles of operant conditioning and schedules of reinforcement.

Mathetics Programming

In programmed instruction the presentation of the instructional material or subject matter to the learner in a suitable form is termed as programming. Various types of programming have emerged on account of researches and experimental studies in the field of programmed instruction. One such type is mathetics programming. This style of programming has been propagated by Thomas F. Gilbert (1962). In the words of Gilbert "mathetics is defined as a systematic application of reinforcement theory to the analysis and construction of complex repertoires which represent the mastery of subject matter".

Though quite technical in its approach this style proves quite helpful in learning difficult skills, shaping desired behaviour and acquiring complete mastery over the subject matter.

In this style, an exercise is the technical unit of learning. No restriction is put on the size of extent of an exercise. Its size is determined not by 'breaking the material into small parts' but by determining how big a step a learner can reasonably take at the moment. This programme makes use of the technique of 'Retrogressive or backward chaining. In order to develop the problem - solving skill of the students mathetics programming technique was adopted in the *CAI* package on 'Double Integrals'.

This chapter gives the necessary background for the Computer Assisted Instruction with many details about computer in general and computer Assisted Instruction in particular. The effectiveness of *CAI*, found out by many researchers so far, is discussed in the succeeding chapter.

CHAPTER 3

REVIEW OF RELATED LITERATURE

INTRODUCTION

Review of literature pertaining to a problem makes the researcher familiar with the summary of previous research, the writing of recognized experts, what is already known, and what is still unknown and untested and thus provides a background for the development of the study undertaken. "This step helps to eliminate the duplication of what has been done, and provides useful hypotheses and helpful suggestions for significant investigation" (Best, 1974). This brings the researcher to the proximity of the solution. It is in this context, that studies on Computer Assisted Instruction in Mathematics and the variables that affected the effectiveness of *CAI* are reviewed in the following pages in view of their relevance to the present study.

REVIEW OF RELATED LITERATURE

The first computer language was developed by Seymour Papert called LAGO in the Massachusetts Institute of Technology in USA. (Papert,S. 1980).

Harding (1982) suggested that Australian school leaving girls showed better average scores in tests of Mathematics and exhibited a better average performance in the computing skills.

The under achievement of women in Computer Sciences especially in the fields of problem solving was reported. (Kay and Prosser 1983).

It has been observed by Kay and Prosser (1983) and Konvalina *et. al.* (1983) that higher secondary school Mathematics programme is correlated with success in the learning of computer courses.

Girls were reported to be timid when facing the computer and they had very low self image on being introduced to a computer (Williams and Pepe, 1983).

Sex differences in Mathematics and computer achievement were reported by Erickson and Erickson (1984). Among many of the advantages of Computed Aided Instruction, the integrity among participants is given more weightage (Lane and Lane, 1984). It is also observed that students engage themselves in more discussion while learning and interact enthusiastically in their class rooms. Computers when used in the class rooms encourage teacher-pupil dialogue.

The first and foremost introduction of computers in the classroom was reviewed by Alison (1985). It was reported that computers were incorporated in the regular school curriculum and made the process of learning exciting and enjoyable for the young students in USA.

But whatever may be the credit contributed to computers and *CAI*, the computers will and can probably act only as a Teaching Assistant rather than substitute the teacher as such. Knotos (1985) found that computers support the teachers in the creation of an environment with many improved opportunities for learning. On the basis of an interview conducted, Lockhel (1985) observed that men generally liked more the *CAI*/CAL programmes than women. But lack of self-confidence in male dominated group was observed by the same author. It is observed by Barren et al (1985) that proportion of women entering computer courses have dropped significantly, suggesting that computer courses at the higher secondary level in Britain do not encourage girls to pursue the same. Powles (1986) reported negative consequences regarding the discouragement by the parents of the girls for pursuing the computer science courses. Hawkins (1986) reported that more women than men achieved grade at the computer graduation class. Kay *et al* (1986) reported that computing is commonly seen and presented as heavily technology centred and reliant upon Mathematics. These authors found that the Computer Aided Instruction Programmes provided some pre-programming skills which enhanced the confidence of women to perform better.

The miracle and means of using computers in the Mathematics education was debated in one of the international congress of Mathematical education. (Burkhard and Davis, 1986). These authors have mentioned that days are not far off when computers are must for teaching of Mathematics.

In India only during 1986 the usage of microcomputers in the learning of Science was suggested and the effectiveness of CAL was also cited (Srinivasa Raghavan 1986).

But since then the Computer Literacy Programme (CLASS) is well understood by many of the Indian Schools, thanks to Ministry of Human Resource Development, Government of India. Moreover in the general stream of Education, introduction of computer sciences in the Higher Secondary Schools in Tamil Nadu and many other state Boards (Higher Secondary) of Education has paved the way for the improved planning and thinking. The interaction between the Computer Aided Learners and teachers were well specified in a (Srinivasaraghavan, 1986) booklet and as stated by the same author, the students might improve well by learning computer programmes and its applications to everyday life, since computers have now been accepted as an indispensable extension of human intellect in science learning.

The impact of computers and informatics on mathematics education and research especially with respect to the learning and teaching of mathematics were brought out very elaborately by Kapur (1987). He stressed and brought the insights into mathematical modelling as a next step of clubbing mathematics and computer education.

The influence of computer and informatics on Mathematics and its teaching has been well documented by Brehlar (1987) and the same was discussed in one of the international symposiums (Howson and Kahane, 1987).

The usage of computers and calculators in Mathematics Education in India to cater to the fulfillment of the new education policy (NEP) was stressed and detailed (Kapur, 1988).

Computer Assisted Learning and its efficiency in Medicine was also illustrated by Pieme (1988). It was argued here that at least the teachers are sure that their students are awake. Callison (1988) listed the uses of micro computes in mathematics education in any classroom and stated that this added a new dimension of richness to one's teaching and learning. The reform of the high school education in Russia and the achievements and difficulties of the remodelling of higher education – with respect to the computerisation strategy in USSR were very lucidly brought out by Saveiyan and Venua (1989).

A clarion call for the need for encouraging women and girl students for learning mathematics was given by Kapur, 1990. He clarified the doubt that mathematics especially mathematics education is difficult for girls. Extensive research in various western institutions has proved decisively that there is no intrinsic difference in the learning capacities of boy and girl students.

Phalavonk (1991) of University of New South Wales investigated achievement and motivational effects of Computer Assisted Instruction (*CAI*) for University Mathematics. The population of the study consisted of the 1989 first-year science or applied science students who enrolled in a compulsory Mathematics subject at Government Universities in Thailand.

Two experimental groups were formed. Each group studied one topic through *CAI*. The control group was taught a new topic through traditional classroom method. A non-*CAI* group was taught both topics by traditional lecture method. The achievement and attitude/interest scores of the experimental students were found to be significantly higher than those of the control students. Additional results indicated that *CAI* produced better achievement levels for all students independently of their sex, high-school mathematics grade level, previous computer experience, and intended major field. However, a more positive attitudinal changes towards mathematics was produced by *CAI* in male students.

Jayathilakan (1992) found out that there was no interaction effect between intelligence and the method of teaching on the achievement of the learners.

The role of computers in education was observed by Venkatasubramanian (1992) and he presented a fine article advocating the case of computerisation. At the present stage it is very difficult to forecast what the developments in the computerisation will be, since the situation at present is very fluid and developing rapidly.

Sarasa (1992), in her study, 'Effectiveness of Computer Assisted Instruction in the Learning of Mathematics of Higher Secondary Girls' found out that the students learning through computer Assisted Instruction performed better than the students taught through traditional method in Mathematics.

Fredenbergs (1993) of Montana State University tried to explore the use of *CAI* in a traditional college course. For this study, the experimental group consisted of four sections of Math 181 : Calculus and Analytic Geometry I, at Montana State University. Students in this group were administered five weeks in highly visual and supplemental laboratories. The control group consisted of four other sections of the same course, and was administered five corresponding supplemental homework assignment.

The independent and attribute variables were treatments and learning style, gender, and minority group membership. The dependent variables were student attitudes, anxiety and achievement. These variables were assessed through changes in pre-treatment and post treatment surveys and student scores on homework, quizzes and exams, and course grades.

Results indicated little statistically significant change in student attitudes and anxiety, and no statistically significant change in achievement. Students receiving supplemental computer labs performed as well as students who received additional home work.

Recommendations for further research include; continued research into the use of supplemental *CAI* in the form of computer labs; research into the use of graphing calculators in college calculus; research into long term effects of *CAI* in college calculus; and research into college calculus courses which have been restructured to take advantages of technology in the classroom.

Shiah (1994) of Purdue University studied the effects of Computer Assisted Instruction on the Mathematical Problem-Solving of students with Learning Disabilities. Four Major findings were obtained. First, students in all conditions improved significantly on math word problem solving from pre to post testing. Second, no statistically significant difference were detected among the treatment conditions. Third, students in all conditions performed significantly better on the online computer tests than on paper-and-pencil tests. No evidence of transfer between on-line computer and paper-and-pencil tests was observed. Finally, all students across all conditions reported that they enjoyed using the computer programs and that they enjoyed using the pictures.

Gittinger (1994) of University of Texas at Austin wanted to compare the effectiveness of Computer Assisted Instruction with that of co-operative learning in increasing students' mathematical achievement. The co-operative learning groups registered higher post test scores than the Computer-Assisted Instruction group in ten of the sixteen ethnic-gender –treatment groups, even though six of these ten groups began with lower post-test scores than did their counter parts in the *CAI* group.

Ryan (1994) of University of South Carolina made an attempt to find out the effectiveness of *CAI* while teaching elementary algebra to the students of a community college. The results revealed the following characteristics to be common among the successful Computer Assisted Instruction students:

(i) Students under 25 years of age performed better in the Computer Assisted format than students over 25;

(ii) Minority students performed significantly better in the Computer Assisted format than they did in the traditional classroom; and

(iii) Students of middle or high socio-economic status performed significantly better in the Computer Assisted format than those of lower socio-economic status.

Bohn (1994) of University of Honston compared the mean scores on a final examination between a group of students (19) choosing a *CAI* developmental mathematics course and a group of students (13) choosing the course in the traditional mode. This study was conducted at the south east college of Houston community college system. The quasi-experimental research design used a pre test – post test control group design. The result obtained from the 't' test ($t = 1.10$, $p = .141$) and analysis of covariance ($F = 2.09$, $P = .165$, and $F=0.94$, $P = .342$) indicated that there was no statistically significant difference between the mean scores on the final examination of the two groups.

Tetlock (1995) of the University of Manitoha (Canada) investigated the effects of using a curriculum–based *CAI* program in the mathematics class room. The study examined how the teaching process changed when implementing such a program, and the effect that such a program on students' attitudes towards computer and toward mathematics.

Teacher report forms were developed to help the teachers reflect on their teaching behavior, and on the impact that the software had on their teaching as well as on the students. These reports were qualitative in nature and were completed throughout the duration of the study. Questionnaires consisting of Likert-type statements were developed to assess students' attitude towards computer and towards mathematics. The students also responded to two open-ended questions where they indicated what they liked the most and what they liked the least about using the software in their mathematics class.

A major change in the teaching process was that of a significant role change. The teacher became a facilitator in the learning process. Another major change in the teaching process was in the type of preparation that was needed. Extensive time was spent previewing the software before using it in the class room. Also, teacher activities focusing on hardware and software issues in the class room were new additions to the teaching process. Decisions on pacing and when to supplement the software with instruction presented new challenges to the teachers. The students' attitudes towards computers did not show any significant changes over the course of the study. However, student attitudes towards mathematics showed some significant improvements at the completion of the study compared with the beginning of the study.

Burton (1995) of Grambling State University investigated the effectiveness of Computer Assisted Instruction (*CAI*) versus traditional instruction on the academic performance of adult students on the mathematics and reading sections of the Test of Adult Basic Education (TABE).

Additionally this study investigated the independent influence of the variables age, gender, income, marital status, educational level, ethnicity and the employment status on the academic performance of adult students on the total section of the TABE

The conclusions of this study were as follows:

(i) The type of instruction had an influence on the academic performance of adult students on the maths and reading sections of the TABE.

(ii) Adult students' age had no effect on their total scores on the TABE.

(iii) Male and female adult students had nc similar scores on the total sections of the TABE.

(iv) Ethnicity had some influence on the academic performance of adult students on the total section on the TABE. The more formal education adult students had obtained, the higher their scores were on the total section of the TABE.

Sadatmand (1995) of United States International University investigated the effects of Computer Assisted Instruction on

Algebraic problem solving abilities of Community College students. Statistical evidence in this study supported the findings that Computer Assisted Instruction (*CAI*) can enhance a students' growth in mathematics. Research also indicated that it is possible to improve students' problem solving capabilities at the Elementary Algebra and Intermediate Algebra levels. Although the difference between the experimental Intermediate Algebra and control post-test scores in the intermediate Algebra was not statistically significant, the difference was in the hypothesized direction. The lack of difference may have been due to the significant difference in gender.

Bjarnason (1995) of University of Alberta (Canada) devised strategies for the improvement of Computer Assisted Instruction (*CAI*). The Alberta Education Mathematics materials were used by the urban Full year and Rural semestered classes included in this study.

The strategies focussed on the areas of students' time on task, subjective feed back, and achievement scores. The time on task and subjective feed back data gathered, came from Computer generated student audit trails. The *CAI* teachers supplied the students' achievement scores. Additional data came from observation of the urban full year students.

The strategies for the improvement of the *CAI* stemmed from the findings that in both classes there was a high percentage (48.8%) of low scoring and High-scoring (above 79%) students, on two different diploma examinations. A further analysis of the urban full time students' time on task, subjective feed back and researchers observation of them, served to initiate other strategies.

Chen (1995) of University of Texas at Austin examined the instructional effects of Computer Static graphics, animated graphics, and digital motion video on students' performance and attitude in Computer Assisted Instruction.

A new instructional Computer program on the topic "Earthquakes" was designed to be used as the stimulus material for this study. One control group and three experimental groups of 25 graduate students each were selected as volunteers from a department in a large state University in Texas. The control group received a computer programme with text only; the three experimental groups were groups receiving computer programs with text and static graphics, text and animated graphics and text with digital video motion respectively. The text content for the four versions of instruction was the same. The general hypothesis of this study was that students' achievement test scores and attitude would be significantly higher after receiving a Computer Assisted learning lesson with text and digital motion video.

The results of this study indicate that computer graphics did not make a significant difference in affecting students' academic performance, but they did make a significant difference on subjects' attitude in this study.

Cox (1996) of Oklahoma State University conducted a qualitative study to determine if significant differences existed between the basic skills achievement growth of vocational students enrolled in Oklahoma area vocational technical schools' Education Enhancement centers using two different instructional methodologies. Two groups comprised the study; one was contextually taught the basic skills by having an instructor relate the mathematics or reading basic skills instruction to the vocational program and the other group was taught the basic skills through an integrated learning machine.

The investigator found out that mathematics and reading basic skills achievement scores were significant when a contextual approach was used versus a computer assisted approach for teaching the basic skills.

Collins (1996) of University of South Florida examined the effects of Computer Assisted Algebra instruction on achievement, mathematics anxiety levels, and attitudes toward personal use of computers of students in an historically Black University. Using a 2 (Method) x 2 (Instructor) x 2 (Gender) x 3 (Time) repeated measures design, two classes consisting of a total of 48 undergraduate college students were randomly assigned to the experimental condition (direct classroom instruction combined with computer assisted instruction). All four groups studied the same ten units in an intermediate algebra course, but used two different instructional strategies. The research was designed to test the following hypothesis; Students attending an historically Black University using direct class room instruction combined with Computer Assisted instruction will score significantly higher on the achievement test in algebra, show a significantly greater decrease in mathematics anxiety and show significantly greater positive attitudes toward personal use of computers than students using direct class room instruction without computer assisted instruction.

An analysis of Covariance (ANCOVA) on post–test and follow - up test measures revealed that the instructional treatment produced no significant differences between the experimental and control groups on overall achievement in algebra. Mean achievement scores for the experimental group at pre-test, post-test and follow-up test were 50%, 52%, and 49%, respectively while the control group had mean scores of 44%, 51%, and 49%. The low level of performance for both groups suggests that the time span for the study may have been too short to achieve progress.

The instructional treatment did not produce significant differences between the experimental and control groups on overall mathematics anxiety on the follow-up test. The experimental groups showed less mathematics anxiety than the control groups. No significant differences in mathematics anxiety were observed for males and females. On overall attitudes toward personal use of Computers, significant differences were found between the experimental and control groups on the follow-up test. Students in the experimental group had significantly more positive attitudes toward personal use of computers than the students in the control group.

Rinaldi (1997) of Eastern Michigan University examined the effects of Computer Assisted Instruction (*CAI*) and teacher directed instruction on achievement in Mathematics. The research was designed to determine and evaluate the differences in academic achievement of mathematics students who received *CAI*, as opposed to those who received teacher-directed instruction.

The researcher found that there were no significant differences between the students who received computer assisted instruction, and the students who received direct instruction from the teacher.

French (1997) of Temple University compared the mathematics achievement and attitude towards mathematics of Community College students who were taught pre calculus with interactive computer software (the Treatment) with the mathematics achievement and attitude towards mathematics of students who were taught in a traditional classroom (the control). The type of software used in the study was Mathwright version 1.0. Both quantitative and qualitative methodologies were used in the study. The quantitative measures used were a mathematics achievement test (course final exam) and the Aiken-Dregar Mathematics Attitude Scale (MAS). The statistical analysis of these measures included the use of the student 't' test of significance. For the qualitative investigation of student attitude towards mathematics, a student questionnaire, interviews with a random sample of six students, and observations of students were employed.

The analysis of the results of the quantitative measures of student achievement showed that the Treatment students had significantly more growth in their achievement than the control students; however, there was no statistically significant difference in the gain scores of the two groups. The analysis of the results of the quantitative measures of student attitude towards mathematics showed that there was no statistically significant difference between the MAS scores of the Treatment group versus the control group. However, the analysis of the results of the qualitative measures of student attitude towards mathematics showed that the Treatment students had significantly more positive attitudes towards mathematics than the control students. The conclusions drawn from this study were: (i). The use of interactive computer software does increase the mathematics achievement of students. (ii). The use of interactive computer software does not change the

MAS-measured mathematics attitude of students (iii). The use of interactive computer software does change students' attitude towards mathematics in a positive fashion. Recommendations include replicating the study using alternative types of software and other mathematics courses, such as calculus or algebra.

Issa (1998) provides a summary of the results from research on the effects of multimedia-based safety training conducted by the M.E. Rinker , Sr.School of Building Construction at the University of Florida. The findings indicate multimedia-based, self-paced learning offers very distinct advantages over traditional, instructor lead classroom learning. Both high school and college students exhibited superior retention rates when learning from the multimedia -based materials. Higher scoring students in the classroom showed little difference in either media, while students who tended to score at the low end of the grading scale uniformly scored higher on multimedia-based materials.

Antony Maciocia (1999) mentioned that several higher education institutions in Scotland initiated a program that aims to investigate ways and means of sharing teaching materials by making use of computer-aided learning software and direct methods of collaborative teaching. The result of this program is a system called Mathpool. MathPool is a system for centrally storing material for teaching mathematics and is available to the participating universities over an asynchronous transfer mode (ATM) metropolitan area network.

Edwin Christmann and John Badgett (1999) did the research entitled, 'A Comparative Analysis of the Effects of Computer-Assisted Instruction on Student Achievement in Differing Science and Demographical Areas'. This study compared science students who were exposed to traditional methodology with those who received traditional methodology supplemented with computer-assisted instruction (*CAI*). From the 24 conclusions, an overall mean effect size of 0.266 was calculated, indicating that on the average, students receiving traditional instruction supplemented with *CAI* attained higher academic achievement than did 60.4% of those receiving only traditional instruction.

The effect sizes were categorized into four subject areas. In descending order, the mean effect sizes in general science, physics, chemistry, and biology are: 0.707, 0.280, 0.085, and 0.042, respectively

Differences in educational settings revealed that *CAI* is most effective among science students in urban areas followed by those in sub urban areas, and weakest among rural students.

Joy f. Xin of Rowan University, U.S.A.(2000) did a study, "Integrating Technology into Instruction in an Inclusive Classroom for Diverse". In this study, three instructional strategies: team teaching, cooperative learning, and computer assisted instruction, were combined and implemented in an inclusive 3rd grade classroom. Students worked in co-operative learning groups in class and in pairs on the computers. A regular education and a special education teacher engaged in team teaching. Three commercially produced computer software packages covering computation and problem solving were utilized. The results of the study show that special and regular education students acquire mathematics skills together successfully when the strategies are research based, motivating, and effectively accommodate diversity than those receiving only traditional instruction.

Monica (2001) conducted the research in two geometry classrooms to determine whether the use of a multimedia instructional strategy could increase learning. The multimedia group members used PowerPoint to make their presentations, while the traditional group used the marker board, paper and pencil to make their presentations. Observation, a presentation rubric, and a focus group were used to collect data for this study. A total of 39 students from two geometry classes participated in the study. Results indicated that both groups of students increased geometry concept learning when they used both a visual and verbal explanation, rather than a verbal explanation alone. The multimedia group scored higher than the traditional group when they were given ample time to learn how to use PowerPoint. It was determined that students should be given an opportunity to give both a visual and verbal explanation of geometry topics. They should also be given enough time to learn the multimedia program before using it. Another implication is that teachers should group students who have little knowledge of technology with more knowledgeable students and integrate technology across the curriculum. The results of the study were presented to teachers in the math department and administrators. A PowerPoint presentation was used to report the findings and implications, and to display presentations made by the participants of the study. Teachers were instructed on how they could use the multimedia strategy in their classroom.

Fletcher Debbie (2001) did a research to determine the effectiveness of computer-assisted instruction as review preparation for high-stakes tests in mathematics. An instructional unit was taught to ten eleventh-grade students over a two-week time span. Five participants reviewed using computer-assisted instruction and five participants were taught using traditional instruction. This qualitative study included observation, interviews, pre- and post-intervention surveys, and pre- and post-intervention practice versions of the Georgia High School Graduation Test. Findings suggest that review will improve Georgia High School Graduation Test scores, particularly using computer-assisted instruction. Participants indicated that the review is of value and should be continued. The results of the study were communicated to the learning community through a meeting with teachers and administrators. This meeting supported beginning test review as early as the tenth grade.

Fionnuala Flanagan (2002) did a study, "Mathematics An Educational Enquiry into the use of Concept Mapping and Multimedia to Enhance the Understanding of Mathematics " in School of Computer Applications, Dublin City University. This dissertation investigates the potential that concept mapping and the multimedia software Flash4.0 have for enhancing students' understanding of Mathematics. It focuses on developing the students, problem-solving skills through use of concept mapping. The structuring of their solutions in a logical diagrammatic format through concept mapping will enable them to animate their Mathematical solutions through use of Flash4.0, thus creating a representation of their understanding of the maths problem.

The participants in the study were a mixed gender class selected from Transition Year in the Irish second level education system. On the basis of the level that they took for their Junior Certificate Examination, Honours and Ordinary level groups were formed. Each group was ranked according to their Mathematical aptitude, identified from the results of Differential Aptitude Tests which measure: Numerical Ability, Abstract Reasoning, Mechanical Ability and Space Relations. They were then allocated into homogenous pairs, thus creating a collaborative learning environment.

An Action Research study was undertaken. Both groups took part in six sessions, presented over a three-week period, designed to develop, explore and examine the areas mentioned above, providing a more progressive methodology for the teaching of Mathematics. An evaluation of the study was formed based on the evidence gathered from student journals; their practitioner's diary, video and audio tapes, questionnaires, learning styles tests, concept maps, and animations created in Flash 4.0. Both groups were pre- and post-tested using Mathematics question and those sections from the Differential Aptitude Tests that were mentioned above. The results showed that this methodology created an environment that enabled the students to develop positive attitudes towards Mathematics. Concept mapping and the use of multimedia motivated them to become active participants in their own learning process, increased their confidence in the problem-solving cycle, and facilitated the perception of Mathematics through their 'eyes'. The findings show that both the Honours and Ordinary level students improved in Abstract and Mechanical reasoning, and Space relations as a result of this enquiry. However the degree of improvement achieved by the Ordinary level students compared to the Honours students was significant. This methodology enhanced the student's enjoyment, understanding, and appreciation of Mathematics.

Several researches have been undertaken to find out the effect of Computer Assisted Instruction on mathematics at school level. But only a few researches have been carried out to study the effect of *CAI* on teaching mathematics at higher education level. Hence this research has been undertaken to find out the effect of Computer Assisted Instruction on teaching of "Double Integrals" at undergraduate level.

CHAPTER 4

RESEARCH PROCEDURE

INTRODUCTION

This chapter deals with the research procedure related to *CAI* (Computer Assisted Instruction) for undergraduate students on 'Double Integrals'. The success of any programme of education depends upon systematic research which could generate statistical, descriptive and analytical information for effective implementation for continuous assessment. In the case of innovative programmes, the need for a series of research studies to build up an empirical basis cannot be over emphasized.

Studies reviewed in the previous chapter do not exclusively point to the superiority and utility of *CAI* programe for teaching mathematics to students of undergraduate classes. Hence, the researcher wanted to find out the efficacy of a *CAI* program with particular reference to the first year undergraduate students who have opted mathematics as a major or an allied subject.

RESEARCH PARADIGM

The present study intends to study the effectiveness of *CAI* on Double Integrals over conventional teaching with regard to students' achievement. Apart from determining the effect of

CAI, the preferences over the two methods viz., *CAI* and conventional instruction of the students are also to be ascertained. The prominent factor which influences the achievement level of the students when they learn 'Double Integrals' through *CAI* is to be studied. The factors considered for the purpose of the study are family income, educational level of the father, educational level of the mother and family size.

A pilot study was conducted to ascertain the preferences over the two methods of instruction. Preference indices were framed using 'Pilot Survey – Forced Distribution of weightage'. In order to determine the effectiveness of *CAI*, Pre and Post experimental design was followed.

SAMPLE FRAME

The students at the undergraduate level opting for mathematics either as a major or as an allied subject in the Bharathidasan University, Tamil Nadu formed the universe of the study. The students studying in Jamal Mohamed College, Tiruchirappali, Tamil Nadu constituted the sample for the study. 282 students were selected for this purpose. Systematic Random sampling method was used for sample selection. There were 168 students in the experimental group and 114 students in the control group. The features of the sample are given in the Table 1.

Table 1
Distribution of the Sample

	Sex		*Language of Instruction*		*Locale*		
Group	*Male*	*Female*	*Tamil*	*English*	*Rural*	*Urban*	*Group-wise total*
Experimental	105	63	43	125	36	132	168
Control	57	57	34	80	34	80	114
Total	162	120	77	205	70	212	282

VARIABLES SELECTED FOR THE STUDY

The treatment variables were the teaching techniques namely

(a) *CAI* technique and

(b) Conventional method of teaching

The independent variables were sex, locale, language of instruction, family income, father's' education, mother's education and size of the family.

The dependent variable was "Achievement of the students".

SOURCE MATERIALS

The investigator had gone through the prescribed text books, reference books, books dealing with Teaching of Mathematics, magazines, reports, booklets on the development of structured software packages and reviewed some of the available *CAI* packages. With the knowledge gained from the above, the investigator made thorough analysis of the contents of the selected units and then developed the *CAI* package on this topic. The lecturers handling the first year Mathematics classes were also contacted and the difficulties encountered by them while teaching the unit were also taken into consideration.

TOOLS USED

The tools used by the researcher consisted of the *CAI* software developed by the investigator, achievement tests for pre and post tests developed by the investigator, Mathetics programming propagated by Gilbert to develop problem solving skill by the learners in the *CAI* package, and the 'Personal Data Blank' to collect data from the sample students.

In this study, z - test to analyse the differential hypotheses, F - test to find out the interaction effect, Correlation - test, Stepwise Multiple Regression Analysis using SPSS package and ANOVA - techniques were the statistical techniques applied to draw the conclusions.

ACHIEVEMENT TEST

In order to prepare achievement test, the relevant books on 'Tests & Measurements' were referred and suggestions from experienced Professors of Mathematics were sought. Keeping in mind the objectives specified, the test items were constructed on the topic 'Double Integrals'. In consultation with the experts from the fields of mathematics and education, due weightages were given to the instructional objectives viz., Knowledge, Understanding, Application and Skill.

Validity and Reliability of the Achievement Test

Before constructing the test items, the researcher has gone through the important source materials and opinions obtained from experienced lecturers and professors regarding the adequacy of test items in terms of marks to be given to each unit and identified objectives in the content and behavioural outcomes regarding units in content. Due weightages have been given to major objectives of teaching 'Double Integrals' viz., 'Knowledge', 'Understanding', 'Application' and 'skill' to the unit specified.

The reliability of the achievement test on the selected topic 'Double Integrals' for first year undergraduate students, was determined by Split Half Technique. The reliability coefficient was found to be 0.72 and the reliability of the whole test was calculated using Spearman-Brown Prophecy formula and was found to be (0.84) significant at 0.05 level.

Blue Print of the Achievement Test

The test paper, thus prepared, consisted of 40 items. The items found in the paper were of multiple choice and short answers type. The correct answers for each question carried one mark. The distribution of weightages given in contents and objectives of the question and the blue prints of the achievement test are given in Table 2, 3 and 4 respectively.

Table 2
Distribution of Weightages to Contents

Contents	*Marks / No. of questions*	*Percentage*
Introduction to Definite Integrals	41	10.0
Concept of Double Integrals	31	32.5
Method of evaluation of Double Integrals	11	27.5
Evaluation of iterated integrals	2	30.0
Total	40	100.0

Table 3
Distribution of Weightages to Objectives

Objectives	*Marks / No. of questions*	*Percentage*
Knowledge	14	35
Understanding	10	25
Application	10	25
Skill	6	15
Total	40	100

Table 4
Blue Print of the Achievement Test

Topic	*Knowledge*	*Under-standing*	*Appli-cation*	*Skill*	*Tot. Marks/ Questions*	*Percen-tage*
Introduction to Definite Integrals	1	1	1	1	4	10.0
Concept of Double Integrals	4	3	4	2	13	32.5
Method of Evaluation of Double Integrals	4	3	2	2	11	27.5
Evaluation of iterated integrals	5	3	3	1	12	30.0
Total Marks/Questions	14	10	10	6	40	-
Percentage of Marks/ Questions	35	25	25	15	-	100.0

SOFTWARE DEVELOPMENT

An interactive *CAI* package was developed in order to measure the effectiveness of the Computer Assisted Instruction against the conventional method of teaching "Double Integrals" to the undergraduate students.

The following softwares were used to develop the *CAI* package:

Java Script, Java Applet, HTML 4.0, Corel Draw 9.0, 3D Studio Max, Photo Shop 7.0, Flash 5.0, Corel Image Ready, Auto Cad 2000, Front-Page 2000, MS Word, Xara webstyle etc.

Development of Computer Assisted Instruction for Double Integrals

As the investigator intended to study the effectiveness of *CAI* over conventional method of instruction on 'Double Integrals', an interactive *CAI* package was developed in consultation with subject experts, educational psychologists and software professionals. While developing a *CAI* package, the instructions suggested by Stephen M. Alessi and Stanley R. Trollip (1985) were taken into account. The researcher has adopted the following eight stages in the development of *CAI*.

(i) Define the purpose of the lesson.

(ii) Collect resource materials

(ii) Generate ideas for the lesson

(iv) Organise the ideas for the lesson

(v) Produce lesson displays on paper

(vi) Flowchart the lesson

(vii) Programme the lesson

(viii) Evaluate the quality and effectiveness of the lesson

Defining the Purpose of the Lesson

This stage refers to determining what the investigator wants his students to know or will be able to do at the end of the lesson. A more complete elaboration of very specific learning objectives both at the entry and terminal points of the lesson, is desirable. This will be useful for a number of purposes particularly to clarify the appropriate content and methodology of lesson and to inform students whether the lesson is appropriate for them. Keeping the above in mind as the basis for framing objectives, the investigator identified the entry behaviour and terminal behaviour and determined the characteristics of the selected students.

Entry Behaviour

The entry behaviour of the learners has helped the investigator to proceed the research work in the right direction. Previous knowledge is highly essential as it influences the learning process through *CAI*. The following were the behavioural objectives at the entry level of the learners. To learn "Double Integrals", a learner should:

(a) have the knowledge of continuous functions.

(b) be familiar with different methods of integration of functions of single variable.

(c) be able to evaluate definite integrals.

(d) be familiar with the basic properties of definite integrals.

Terminal Behaviour

The success of any educational programme depends upon the attainability of the 'Terminal' behaviour. In consultation with the experts from the fields of education and Mathematics, the following terminal objectives were framed. After learning the unit 'Double Integrals', a learner will be able to:

(a) define Double Integrals

(b) define Reiemann sum and Double Riemann sum

(c) define Iterated Integrals

(d) establish the relationship between double Riemann sum and 'Double Integrals'

(e) interpret the geometrical meaning of Double Integrals

(f) understand the method of evaluation of Double Integrals

(g) acquire knowledge about the change of order of integration in Double Integrals.

(h) evaluate Iterated Integrals.

(i) acquire the skill of solving problems in 'Double Integrals'.

The general characteristics such as age, medium of instruction at their secondary school, level of computer exposure, family background were collected from the selected respondents with the help of a questionnaire.

Collection of Resource Materials

Resource materials include every item or source of information essential to the instructional development effort. The researcher has used three kinds of research materials; those relevant to the subject matter; those relevant to the instructional development and teaching process; and those relevant to the delivery system for the lesson such as programming language and computers.

Resource materials relevant to the subject matter include any item that contains the actual subject information and that demonstrates ways in which Double Integrals may be taught. These items include text books, original sources, reference materials, technical manuals etc.

Resource materials relevant to instructional development for teaching Double Integrals through *CAI* include texts and manuals about instructional design.

Resource materials relevant to the delivery system of *CAI* for Double Integrals include the computer itself; operation manuals and references, manuals and text books for the programming language.

Generation of Ideas for the Lesson

It is at this stage in the design process that the researcher encountered difficulties. It was far easier to decide what to teach, that is, to define the purpose of instruction. For the generation of creative ideas, the researcher followed the 'brainstorming' procedure.

A small group consisting of subject experts in Mathematics, Computer Science and Educational Teaching was formed and the group produced rapidly as many ideas in a non-evaluative way. Typically a member of the group voiced an idea, then other group members immediately said what came to their minds. Ideas include problems and potential solutions, relating to the teaching - learning of Double Integrals through *CAI*. The group continued to produce as many ideas as possible until the frequency of new ideas decreased and people began to voice only previous stated ideas.

Organization of Ideas

The fourth step in the design and development process involved five activities:

(a) Elimination of all but the best and most relevant ideas from the long list of ideas generated through brainstorming process.

(b) Analysis of the ideas and addition of detail for a full instructional sequence.

(c) Selection of an instructional methodology or methodologies for the lesson.

(d) Decision making about all the instructional factors relevant to the methodologies.

(e) Preliminary arrangements of ideas into a teaching sequence.

The best ideas were selected by eliminating ideas on the basis of students characteristics, subject matter and delivery system limitations from the generated list. Having selected the best ideas, the "task analysis" and "concept analysis", were applied to choose the suitable teaching sequence and procedure for the selected topic 'Double Integrals'. Task analysis is a procedure for analysing the things which a student must learn to do. Concept analysis is a procedure for analyzing the content itself, the information that the student must know.

The instructional methodology for 'Double Integrals' was selected based on the analysis. Instructional factors relevant to the teaching methodology that are to be used were decided. Finally, the ideas were arranged in the form of a teaching sequence for Double Integrals.

Production of Lesson Displays on Paper

In this stage, following sub steps were adopted to develop a *CAI* package on Double Integrals. They were writing and revising the primary text ; writing and revising the secondary text; producing storyboards ie, process of rewriting the information on to pieces of paper, with each piece corresponding to a separate computer screen display ; checking the fit of overlaying displays; drawing and revising graphic displays; checking graphics and simultaneous text for fitting; assembling the storyboards; reviewing the storyboard assembly and making revisions.

Flowcharting of the Lesson

A flow chart is a graphic depiction of the lesson, which shows what happens in the lesson under all possible circumstances. The flow chart and storyboards together provide a complete description of the lesson content and sequence, which are necessary for programming. More time spent on flowcharting, the less time it will take to complete the programming. Further more accurate and updated flowcharts make the changing of programmes relatively easy. The flow chart of the lesson Double Integrals was designed and used for the development of the package.

Programming the Lesson

Programming a lesson consisted of several steps. The investigator started to code the lesson, based on the entry level and terminal level objectives. The investigator took care to make the code to perform as required, and make it easy to test. Graphics and animations were used in the lesson in order to improve instruction and not to impress the learners. Once the program was written, it was checked for errors using a number of debugging procedures.

Evaluation of the Lesson

The lessons were evaluated in three phases. The first phase in the evaluation process was the quality review phase. To assist in this process, a quality review checklist was used. This checklist comprised of the following parts - language and grammer; surface features of the displays; questions and menus; invisible functions of the lesson; the subject matter and off-line materials.

The second phase in the evaluation process was the pilot-testing. Pilot testing is the process of having representatives of the target population used to test the lesson while monitoring their progress and performance. Pilot testing in this study consisted of the following processes–selecting the helpers; explaining the procedures to them; finding out how much of the subject matter they know already; observing and asking them to go through the lesson; interviewing them afterwards and revising the lesson.

The final phase in the evaluation process was the validation of the lesson, which involved the process of checking how well the lesson worked in a real instructional setting. In other words, in the validation phase the effectiveness of the instruction was evaluated against the objectives of the lesson and comparison to conventional methods of teaching.

These phases have been incorporated in the development of *CAI* package on 'Double Integrals'.

Development of Problem–Solving Skill

Apart from this, the researcher applied one of the 'programmed instruction' techniques viz., 'mathetics programming' in *CAI* to develop problem solving skills' in the learners on "Double Integrals'.

Five basic steps were identified to evaluate iterated integrals. The researcher attempted to teach the method of evaluation of iterated integrals by making use of 'mathetics programming', through seven worked out problems.

All the five steps were exposed to the learners through the first worked out problem.

In the second worked out problem, all the steps except the last, were exposed to the learners. The last step was released to the learners for providing answer.

In every subsequent worked out problem, one additional step from last, was released to the learners for providing answers. The learners would not be permitted to move to the next step, until correct answers were arrived. Whenever the learners couldn't arrive at the answers, they were provided with suitable hints.

In this way the complete mastery of the problem solving skill was developed in learners, through 'mathetics programming' technique.

CONTENTS OF *CAI* PACKAGE ON DOUBLE INTEGRALS

In the first chapter the concepts of definite integrals of single variable, Riemann sum, the geometrical meaning of definite integrals were introduced to the learners.

Based on the concepts introduced in the first chapter, the concept of 'Double Integration' and its geometrical meaning were taught through two dimensional and three dimensional animated graphics, in the second chapter.

The concept of iterated integrals, change of order of integration, method of evaluation of double integrals were explained to the learners through suitable three dimensional animations, in the third chapter.

In the fourth chapter, the researcher applied the technique 'mathetics programming' to provide complete mastery over the 'method of evaluation of iterated integrals'.

This CAI package has the following advantages:

(a) The package runs on any platform which supports GUI (Graphical User Interface)

(b) To use this package no additional software is needed.

(c) To use this package no previous software or hardware knowledge is required.

(d) It is interactive and user friendly.

(e) It is easily updatable (like templates)

(f) As this package is available in .html, it requires less memory for execution. Moreover it occupies less storage space.

The minimum hardware and software requirements to use the *CAI* package on 'Double Integrals' are given below:

Hardware requirements (minimum)

CPU	:	Pentium IV
RAM	:	64 MB
Hard Disk	:	20 GB
Monitor	:	SVGA colour monitor
Mouse	:	Freehand mouse

Software requirements (minimum)

Internet Explorer version 6.0/5.0

Windows NT/2000/98

The *CAI* package developed is placed as annexure in a CD and the copies of the printed programme are presented in the following pages.

DEFINITE INTEGRALS -A REVIEW

(Introduction to Definite Integrals)

Hello, dear learner, let me welcome you to this package which teaches you the *concepts of double integrals.*

I hope that you are familiar with *integrals involving single variable, definite integrals, their symbols, definitions and integral values* of some basic mathematical functions.

Aren't you ?

Any how, I don't want to take the risk of developing the concepts of double integrals on the basis that you are familiar with the fundamental concepts of integrals.

For that, shall we recall the definitions of integrals of functions of a single variable?

Suppose that f(x) is continuous and is defined for all values of x in the interval $a \leq x \leq b$. Let us divide this interval [a,b] into n sub-intervals $[a, x_1], [x_1, x_2], \ldots, [x_{n-1}, b]$ of equal width say Δx.

Press for figure

FIGURE : 01

Shall I ask a question in this regard ?

Now tell me the value of Δx. (Choose the correct answer)

○	(a - b) / n
○	(b - a) / n
○	(b - a) / (n-1)

Next Page2 Page3

Prev. Next Page1 Page3

Therefore, we have $\Delta x = x_1 - a = x_2 - x_1 = \ldots = b - x_{n-1}$
Is it correct ?

As a special case, let us consider $f(x) \geq 0$. So, the curve $y = f(x)$ lies above the x-axis.

Is it correct ?

Press for figure

FIGURE : 02

Choose sample points $x_1^*, x_2^*, \ldots, x_n^*$ in each of the sub-intervals $[a, x_1]$, $[x_1, x_2]$, ... , $[x_{n-1}, b]$.

Press for figure

FIGURE : 03

Can you imagine the shapes of $f(x_1^*)$, $f(x_2^*)$, ..., $f(x_n^*)$?

Yes. They are nothing but the heights of the curve $y = f(x)$ from the points x_1^*, x_2^*, ..., x_n^* respectively.

Press for figure

FIGURE : 04

Then what do you mean by the quantity $f(x_i^*)\Delta x$?

Prev. Next Page1 Page3

Definite Integrals - A Review

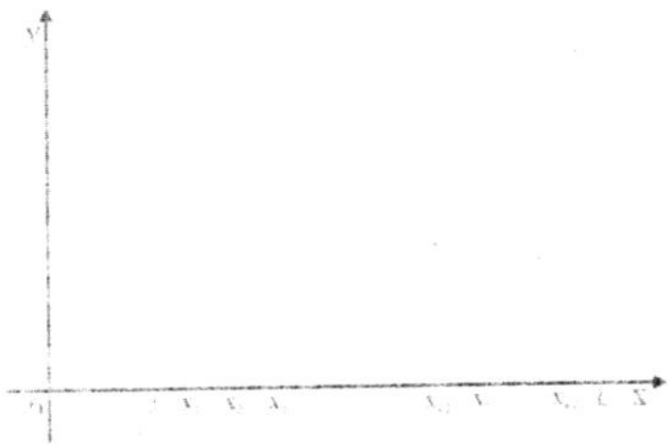

Figure: 01

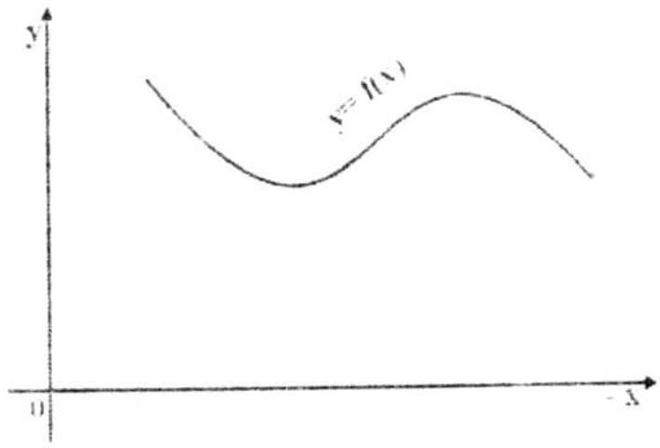

Figure: 02

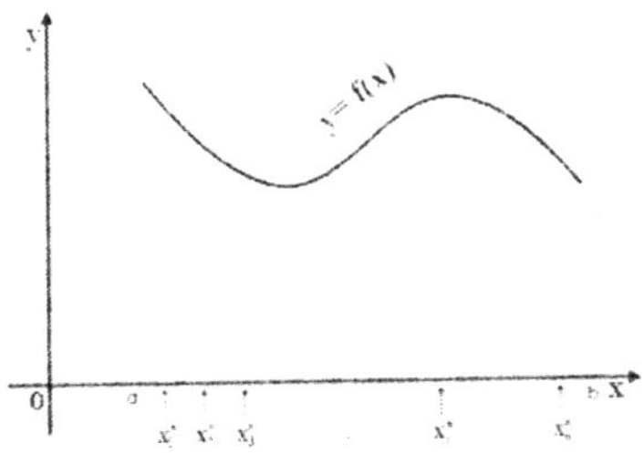

figure: 03

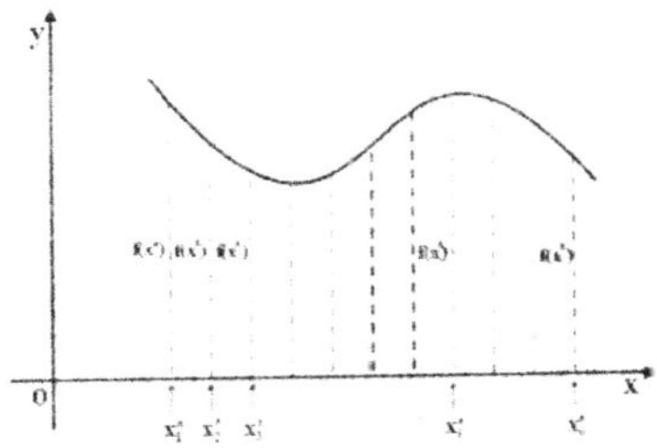

figure: 04

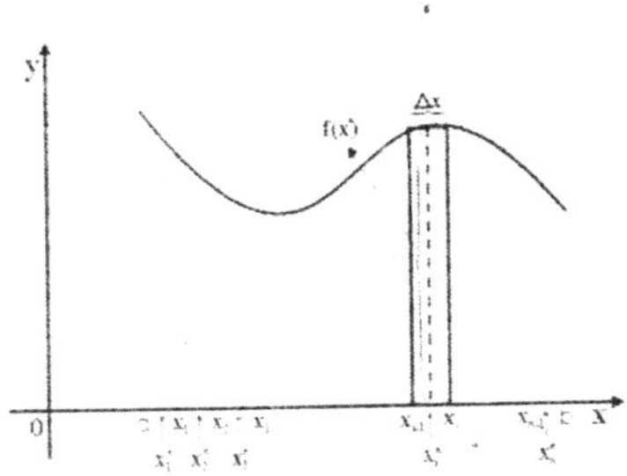

figure: 05

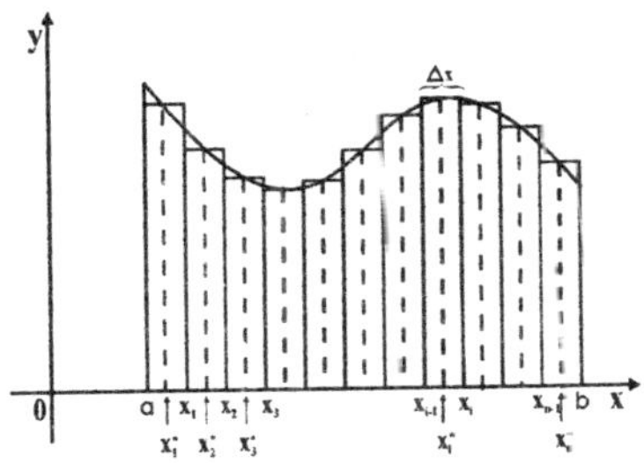

figure: 06

figure: 07

Prev. Page1 Page2

Yes, it is the product of the base length and the height.

Press for figure

FIGURE : 05

Therefore, the quantity $f(x_i^*)\Delta x$ represents... (Choose the correct answer)

- ○ Area of a triangle
- ○ Area of square
- ○ Area of a rectangle

Now, let us form the sum of such quantities for all the sub-intervals.

i.e. $\sum_{i=1}^{n} f(x_i^*)\Delta x$ – which is called the Riemann sum.

How does the above sum look geometrically?

Press for figure

FIGURE : 06

When you look at the figure, you infer that the Riemann sum almost covers the area enclosed by the curve y = f(x) and the x-axis from the line x = a to x = b.

You may wonder why we have used the word 'almost'!

Yes. When you look at the figure, apart from the exact area enclosed by the curve y = f(x), there are some projected areas which are included and some areas which are left out while forming the Reimann sum.

Is it correct?

Press for figure

FIGURE : 07

Now, let us make 'n' very large.

In this case, what will happen to the size of each rectangle ?

They become very small so that all the rectangles together will cover the entire area.

Hence by allowing 'n' tends to infinity, the Riemann sum can be made to cover the whole area enclosed by the curve $y = f(x)$, the lines $x = a$, $x = b$ and the x-axis.

Is it correct ?

Press for figure

FIGURE : 08

If you look at the figure, you will understand how the smaller rectangles cover the entire area when the number of rectangles i.e., 'n' is allowed to become very large.

In this case, we call the Riemann sum as the definite integral of f(x) from a to b, i.e. in symbols,

$$\int_a^b f(x)\,dx = \lim_{n \to \infty} \sum_{i=1}^{n} f(x_i^*)\Delta x$$

In the similar manner, when $f(x) < 0$ for all x lying in the interval [a, b], we can prove that the area bounded by the curve $y = f(x)$ and the x-axis from the line $x = a$ to $x = b$ is given by $-\int_a^b f(x)dx$

Thus, the definition for definite integral applies to all continuous functions f(x).

Definite Integrals - A Review Ends Prev. Page1 Page2

Next Chapter

Definite Integrals - A Review

figure: 08

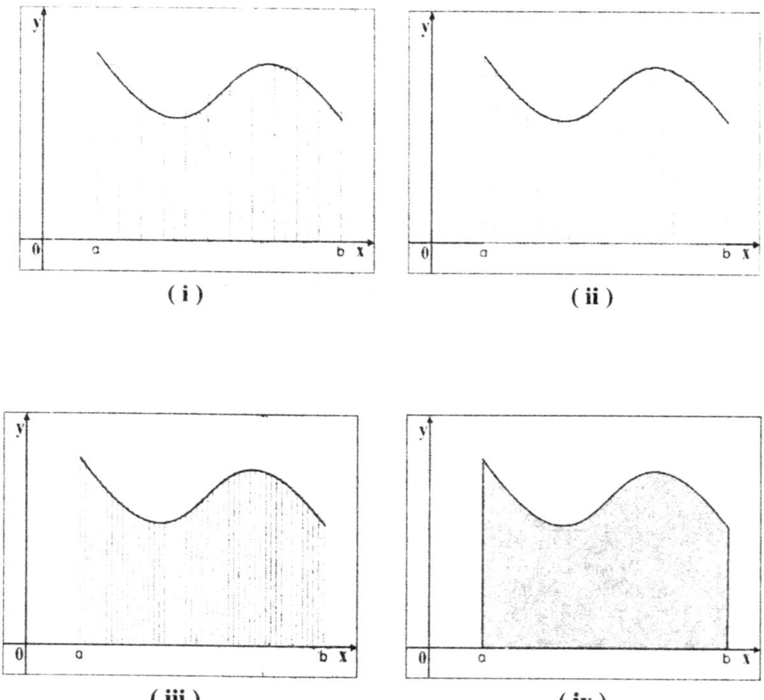

DOUBLE INTEGRALS

(Concept of Double Integrals)

Pre.Chap. Next Page2 Page3 Page4

Dear student, let me recall the definition of definite integral once again:

"If f(x) is a continuous function defined in the interval $a \le x \le b$, then

$$_a\int^b f(x)\,dx = \lim_{n\to\infty} \sum_{i=1}^{n} f(x_i^*)\Delta x$$

Now, we follow the same approach to define the definite integrals of functions of two variables.

Shall we proceed ?

Let us suppose that the function f(x, y) is continuous and is defined on the closed rectangle R given by $R = \{ (x, y) / a \leq x \leq b, \ c \leq y \leq d\}$.

Moreover, let us assume that $f(x, y) \leq 0$.

Can you imagine the surface z = f(x,y) ? .

Yes, the graph of f(x, y) is a surface lying above the xy-plane.

Now look at the following figure.

Press for figure

FIGURE : 01

I hope that you have understood the area of definition of f(x, y) and its surface.

Aren't you ?

Dear learner, now, recall the definition of definite integral of single variable and its geometrical meaning. This will help you in learning double integrals.

Shall we proceed ?

Divide the rectangle R into a number of equal sub-rectangles. This can be done by dividing the interval [a, b] into 'm' sub-intervals $[a, x_1]$, $[x_1, x_2]$, ... , $[x_{m-1}, b]$ of equal width Δx and dividing the interval [c, d] into 'n' sub-intervals $[c, y_1]$, $[y_1, y_2]$, ... , $[y_{n-1}, d]$ of equal width Δy.

Prev. Next Page1 Page3 Page4

Let us form sub-rectangles by drawing lines parallel to the co-ordinate axes through the end points of the sub-intervals.

Shall we name them ?

Yes, let us call them as R_{11}, R_{21}, ... , R_{ij} ......

Can you define the sub-rectangle R_{11} ?

Yes. R_{11} is defined as $R_{11} = \{ (x, y) / a \leq x \leq x_1, c \leq y \leq y_1 \}$

Similarly, R_{21} is defined as $R_{21} = \{ (x, y) / x_1 \leq x \leq x_2, c \leq y \leq y_1 \}$

In genearal, R_{ij} is defined as $R_{ij} = \{ (x, y) / x_{i-1} \leq x \leq x_i, y_{j-1} \leq y \leq y_j \}$

Do you want to view the above sub-rectangles?

Press for figure

FIGURE : 02

As each of the sub-rectangles have the same area, let us denote the area of each sub-rectangles by ΔA.

Now, let me ask a question.

What is the value of ΔA ? (Choose the correct answer)

○ $\Delta x. \Delta x$
○ $\Delta x. \Delta y$
○ (b - a) . (d - a)

Let us choose a sample point in each of the sub-rectangles.

Let us suppose that (x_{ij}^*, y_{ij}^*) be the sample point chosen in the sub-rectangle R_{ij}.

Then, $f(x_{ij}^*, y_{ij}^*)$ represents the height of the rectangular box with base R_{ij}.

Is it so?

Press for figure.

FIGURE : 03

Now, I hope that you are aware of the fact that the volume of a rectangular-box is the product of the area of its base and its height.

i.e. Volume of a box = Base area × Height.

Prev. Next Page1 Page3 Page4

Prev. Next Page1 Page2 Page4

Is it correct ?

Now, consider the product of ΔA and $f(x_{ij}^*, y_{ij}^*)$

i.e., $f(x_{ij}^*, y_{ij}^*)\ \Delta A$

What does it represent ?

Yes. It represents the volume of the rectangular box with the base R_{ij}.

Press for figure

FIGURE : 04

If we add the volumes of all the rectangular boxes, we get an approximation to the total volume V enclosed by the surface z = f(x, y) and the region R.

i.e. the approximate value of V is equal to,

$$\sum_{i=1}^{m} \sum_{j=1}^{n} f(x_{ij}^*, y_{ij}^*),\ \Delta A$$

Press for figure

FIGURE : 05

Why do we take double summation ?

Because, for each sub-rectangle, we evaluate f at the chosen point and multiply it by the area of the sub-rectangle and then we add the results.

I hope that you have understood the purpose of double summation.

Shall we proceed further ?

Let us allow m & n to become very larger. Then what will happen to the size of each rectangular boxes ?

Yes. They become very thin.

Also, they cover the entire volume V enclosed by the surface z = f(x,y) and the region R. Is it so ?

Thus, the volume V is given by

$$V = \lim_{m,n \to \infty} \sum_{i=1}^{m} \sum_{j=1}^{n} f(x_{ij}^*, y_{ij}^*) \Delta A$$

Therefore, when we allow m and n to become very large, we get the volume V.

Look at the following figure and understand how we are covering the entire volume V.

Press for animated figure

FIGURE : 06

Thus, when we allow the rectangular boxes to become very finer and finer, the entire volume V is covered.

Now, we make the following definition. The double integral of ' f ' over the rectangle R is defined to be,

$$\iint_R f(x,y)dA = \lim_{m,n \to \infty} \sum_{i=1}^{m} \sum_{j=1}^{n} f(x_{ij}^*, y_{ij}^*) \Delta A$$

From the above, we get the following fact:

When f(x, y) ≥ 0, the volume V of the solid that lies above the rectangle R and below the surface z = f(x, y) is given by,

$$V = \iint_R f(x,y)dA$$

Am I correct ?

Shall we give a name to the double summation

$$\sum_{i=1}^{m} \sum_{j=1}^{n} f(x_{ij}^*, y_{ij}^*) \Delta A?$$

The above double summation is called the double Riemann sum.

Thus if 'f' happens to be a positive function, the double Riemann sum represents the sum of volumes of rectangular-boxes. When we allow the number of rectangular boxes to become very large, we get very finer rectangular strips. In this case, the double Riemann sum becomes an approximation to the volume under the graph.

For better understanding, look at the animated figure once again and understand the concept.

Press for figure

FIGURE : 07

From our discussion, we observe that the volume V of the solid bounded above by the graph of the continuous non-negative function f(x, y) and below by the rectangle R in the xy-plane is given by,

$$V = \iint_R f(x,y)dA \text{ , where } R = \{ (x, y) / a \le x \le b, c \le y \le d \}$$

Shall we move further ?

In the one variable case, we know that, if $f(x) < 0$ for all $x \in [a, b]$, then the area bounded by the graph $y = f(x)$ and the x-axis is given by $-\int_a^b f(x)dx$.

Similarly, if $f(x, y) < 0$ for all $(x, y) \in R$, then the volume of the solid determined by R and the graph $z = f(x,y)$ equals to $-\iint_R f(x,y)dA$.

Hence, the definition of double integral applies to all continuous functions f of two variables.

Is it correct ?

Now, let us recall the definition of double integral.

" The double integral of f(x, y) over the rectangle $R = \{(x,y)/a \le x \le b,\ c \le y \le d\}$ is given by

$$\iint_R f(x,y)dA = \lim_{m,n \to \infty} \sum_{i=1}^{m} \sum_{j=1}^{n} f(x_{ij}^*, y_{ij}^*)\, \Delta A$$

where $(x_{ij}^*, y_{ij}^*) \in R_{ij} = \{ (x, y) / x_{i-1} \le x \le x_i, y_{j-1} \le y \le y_j \}$ "

I'm sure that you can recall the above definition by yourself.

Okay.

Shall we proceed further ?

Double Integrals - Ends Prev. Page1 Page2 Page3

Next Chapter

EVALUATION OF DOUBLE INTEGRALS

(Method of Evaluation of Double Integrals)

Prev. Page1 Page2 Page3

Let us go through the method of evaluation of double integrals.

Consider the double integral

$$V = \iint_R f(x,y)dA, \text{ where } R = \{(x, y)/ a \leq x \leq b, c \leq y \leq d\} \text{ and } f(x, y) \geq 0.$$

To evaluate the above integral, let us consider a fixed point, say $x_0 \in [a, b]$. Then the integral $\int_c^d f(x_0, y)dy$ denotes the area of cross section $A(x_0)$ standing perpendicular to the x-axis at the point x_0.

Look at the figure and understand about $A(x_0)$.

Press for figure

FIGURE : 01

Here, note that

(i) This area i.e. $A(x_0)$ is bounded above by the curve $z = f(x_0,y)$

(ii) $A(x_0)$ stands perpendicular to the x-axis and

(iii) $A(x_0)$ is obtained by considering $x = x_0$ is a fixed point.

Thus when we evaluate the integral $\int_c^d f(x,y)\, dy$ by treating "x" as constant, we get the area of cross section A(x) at each point x lying in the interval $a \leq x \leq b$.

So, when we combine all these cross-sectional areas together

i.e., when we evaluate the integral, $\int_a^b A(x)\,dx$ we get the required volume under the surface $z = f(x, y)$ above the region R.

Press for animated figur

FIGURE : 02

$$\text{Hence, } V = \int_a^b A(x)dx = \int_a^b \left[\int_c^d f(x,y)dy\right]dx$$

The above volume V can also be evaluated as follows:

As we have done earlier, let us fix a point $y_0 \in [c, d]$.

Then, the integral $\int_a^b f(x,y_0)\,dx$ denotes the area of cross-section $A(y_0)$ standing perpendicular to the y-axis at the point $y = y_0$.

Can you imagine it ?

Press for figure

FIGURE : 03

I hope that you have understood the area of cross-section $A(y_0)$.

Haven't you ?

Now, let us evaluate the integral $A(y) = \int_a^b f(x,y)\,dx$, by treating ' y ' as constant.

Thus, A(y) denotes the cross-sectional areas standing perpendicular to the y-axis at each and every point in the interval $c \leq y \leq d$.

Hence, the integral $\int_a^b A(y)dy$ denotes the combination of all the cross-sectional areas A(y) at each and every point in the interval $c \leq y \leq d$.

i.e., $\int_c^d A(y)dy = \int_c^d \left[\int_a^b f(x,y)dx\right]dy$ denotes the volume V enclosed by the surface $z = f(x, y)$ and the region R.

Look at the following figure and understand the concept.

Press for animated figure

FIGURE : 04

To make you to understand the evaluation of double integral geometrically, we have assumed that the function f(x, y) is nonnegative.

Any how, this condition is not at all essential. So, in general let us make the following definition.

If f(x, y) is a continuous function defined on a region by R = { (x, y) / a ≤ x ≤ b, c ≤ y ≤ d }, then

$$\iint_R f(x, y)dA = \int_a^b\int_c^d f(x, y)\, dydx$$
$$= \int_c^d\int_a^b f(x, y)dxdy$$

Shall we give a name to the composition of two integrals ? Here it is.

An integral involving the composition of two or more successive integrations, each with respect to a single variable, is called an "iterated integral".

Dear learner, so far we have discussed the concepts of double integrals and their geometrical meaning.

Aren't we ?

Now, we shall understand the method of evaluation of the iterated integrals.

Are you ready ?

O.K. Let us consider the iterated integral $\int_a^b\int_c^d f(x, y)dydx$

To evaluate an iterated integral, the innermost integral is to be considered first for evaluation.

Therefore, in the given iterated integral the innermost integral $\int_c^d f(x,y)dy$ is to be evaluated first.

Am I correct ?

As we have ' dy ' in the above integral, therefore we have to integrate with respect to y and the limits are to be substituted for y.

But, the integrand is a function of twc variables namely x and y.

Is it so?

So, when we integrate with respect to y, how will you treat the variable x?

Yes, the variable 'x' is to be treated as constant when we integrate with respect to 'y'.

O.K. After evaluating the innermost integral by treating 'x ' as constant, we are left with the quantity which involves 'x ' and/or constants.

Is it right?

Now, we have to integrate this quantity with respect to 'x' and substitute the limits for 'x'.

I hope that you have understood the method.

The similar procedures are to be followed to evaluate the iterated integral $\int_a^b \int_c^d f(x,y)dxdy$

First evaluate the integral $\int_a^b f(x, y)dx$ by treating 'y' as constant and substitute limits for 'x' namely 'a' and 'b'.

Then, integrate this result with respect to 'y' between the limits 'c' and 'd'.

In general, how will you evaluate an iterated integral?

- Consider the innermost integral and evaluate it.
- If you are integrating with respect to a particular variable, treat the remaining variable as constants.
- Then evaluate the next immediate outermost integral.
- Repeat the above procedures till you evaluate all the integrals.

Evaluation of Double Integrals - Ends Prev. Page1 Page2 Page3

Next Chapter

Double Integrals

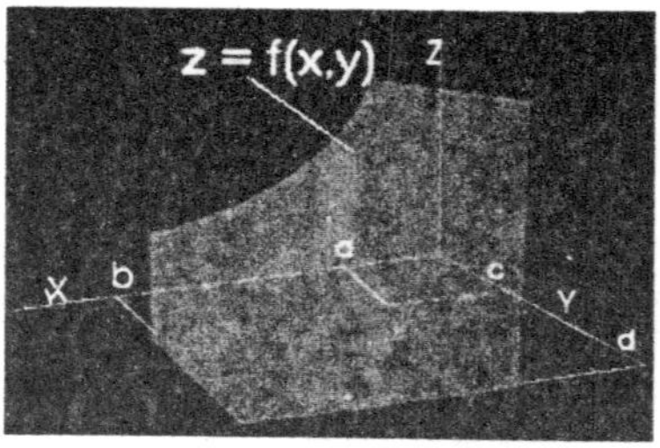

Figure : 01

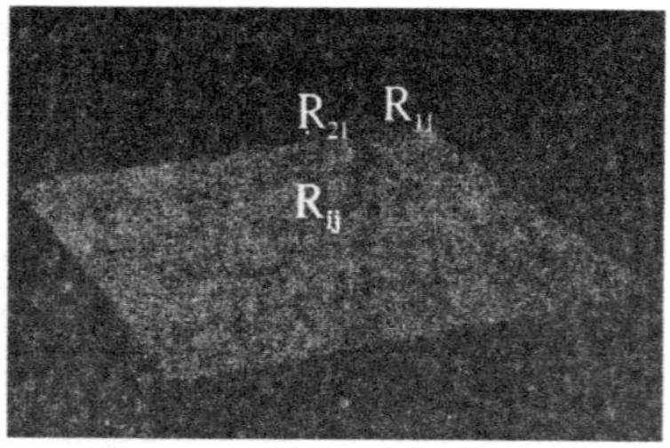

Figure : 02

Figure : 03

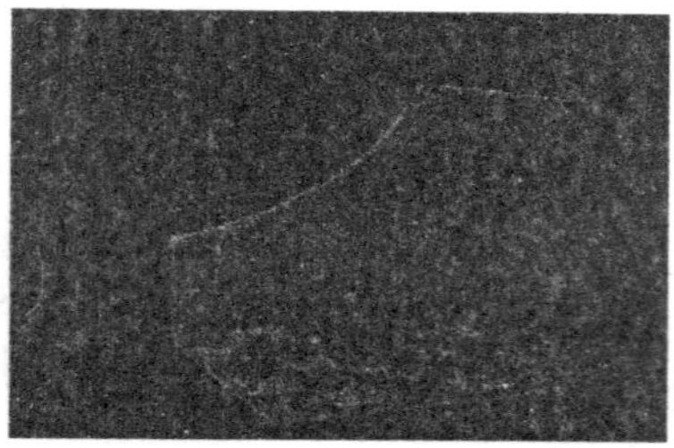

Figure : 04

Figure : 05

Double Integrals

(i)

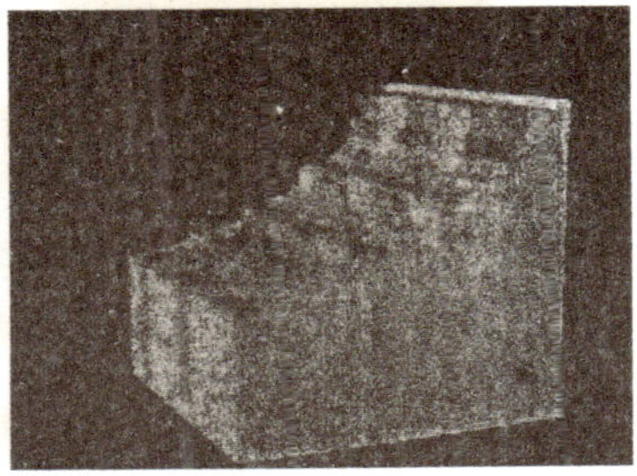

(ii)

(iii)

(iv)

(v)

(vi)

Figure : 06 & 07

Evaluation of Double Integrals

figure : 01

(i)

(ii)

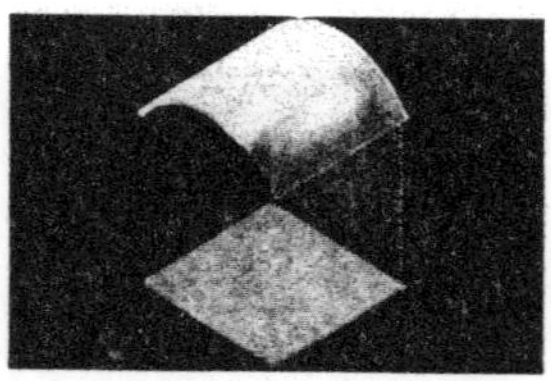

(iii)

(iv)

Figure : 02

Evaluation of Double Integrals

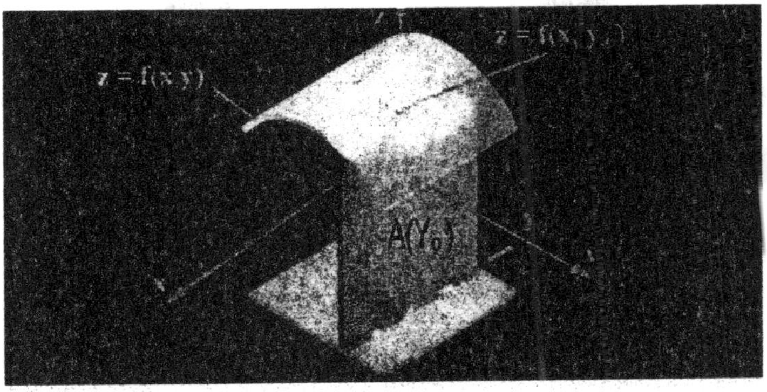

figure : 03

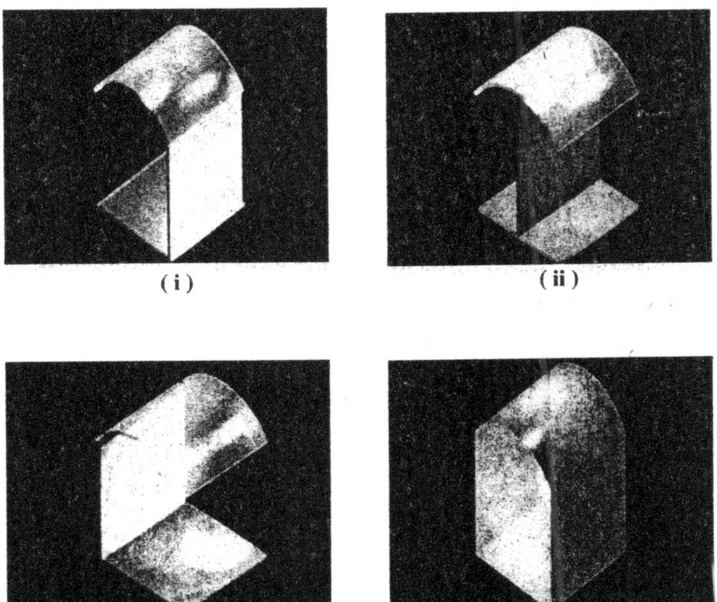

(i) **(ii)** **(iii)** **(iv)**

Figure : 04

EXERCISE

(Evaluation of Iterated Integrals)

Dear Student, before evaluating the double integrals, let me once again recall you the steps involved in the evaluation procedure.

To evaluate the double integral $\int_c^d \int_a^b f(x,y)dxdy$, the procedure to be followed are:

(1) Consider the innermost integral namely $\int_a^b f(x,y)dx$ and evaluate it.

(2) Note that the integral in step-1 is to be integrated with respect to 'x'. Therefore, treat the variable 'y' as constant.

(3) Finally, the result of the integral in step 1 is to be integrated with respect to 'y' between the limits 'c' and 'd'.

Similarly, to evaluate the double integral $\int_a^b \int_c^d f(x,y)dydx$ the procedure to be followed are:

(1) Consider the innermost integral namely $\int_c^d f(x,y)dy$ and evaluate it.

(2) Note that the integral in step-1 is to be integrated with respect to 'y'. Therefore, treat the variable 'x' as constant.

(3) Finally, the result of the integral in step-1 is to be integrated with respect to 'x' between the limits 'a' and 'b'.

I hope that you have understood the above procedure. Aren't you?

Now let us evaluate few double integrals.

EXERCISE : 01

PROBLEM

Evaluate $\int_1^2 \int_3^5 x^3 y^2 \, dx dy$

SOLUTION

Step (1)

Evaluate the innermost integral $\int_3^5 x^3 y^2 \, dx$

Step (2)

As we are integrating with respect to x, treat the variable 'y' as constant.

Step (3)

The value of $\int_3^5 x^3 y^2 \, dx$ is $136y^2$

If you need explanation, press HELP.

Step (4)

Now, integrate the result in Step 3 i.e. $136\,y^2$ with respect to y.

The value of $\int_1^2 136y^2 \, dy$ is 952/3

If you need explanation, press HELP.

Step (5)

Therefore, the value of the given integral namely,

$\int_1^2 \int_3^5 x^3 y^2 \, dx dy$ is 952/3

EXERCISE : 01 Completed

EXERCISE : 02

PROBLEM

Evaluate $\int_1^3\int_1^2 (5+y-x)dxdy$

SOLUTION

Step (1)

Evaluate the innermost integral $\int_1^2 (5+y-x)dx$

Step (2)

As we are integrating with respect to '*x*' treat the variable '*y*' as constant.

(Step 3)

The value of $\int_1^2 (5+y-x)dx$ is $7/2 + y$

If you need explanation, press HELP.

Step (4)

Now, integrate the result in Step-3 i.e. $7/2 + y$ with respect to '*y*'

The value of $\int_1^3 (7/2+y)dy$ is 11.

If you need explanation, press HELP.

Step (5)

Therefore, the value of the given double integral

$\int_1^3\int_1^2 (5+y-x)dxdy$ is ....

(Choose the correct answer)

- ○ 9
- ○ 7/2 + y
- ○ 11
- ○ None of the above

EXERCISE : 02 Completed

EXERCISE : 03

PROBLEM

Evaluate $\int_0^1 \int_0^{\pi/2} x \sin(y) dy dx$

EVALUATION

Step (1)

Evaluate the innermost integral $\int_0^{\pi/2} x \sin(y) dy$

Step (2)

As we are integrating with respect to 'y' treat the variable 'x' as constant.

Step (3)

The value of $\int_0^{\pi/2} x \sin(y) dy$ is x.

If you need explanation, press <u>HELP</u>.

Step (4)

Now, integrate the result 'x' with respect to x.

The value of $\int_0^1 x dx$ is ....

Choose the correct answer.

- ○ x
- ○ 1/2
- ○ $x^2/2$
- ○ 2

Step (5)

The value of the given integral namely,

$\int_0^1 \int_0^{\pi/2} x \sin(y) dy dx$ is ....

Choose the correct answer.

- ○ 1
- ○ 1/2
- ○ $x^2/2$
- ○ 2

EXERCISE : 03 Completed

EXERCISE : 04

PROBLEM

Evaluate $\int_0^1 \int_0^x (y^2 - x^2) dy dx$

EVALUATION

Step (1)

Evaluate the innermost integral $\int_0^x (y^2 - x^2) dy$

Step (2)

As we are integrating with respect to 'y', treat the variable 'x' as constant.

Step (3)

The value of $\int_0^x (y^2 - x^2)dy$ is $2x^3/3$

If you need explanation, press HELP.

Step (4)

Now, integrate the result ______(I) with respect to ______(II).

Choose the correct answer for (I).

- ○ $y^2 - x^2$
- ○ x
- ○ $-2x^3 / 3$
- ○ None of the above

Choose the correct answer for (II).

- ○ x
- ○ y
- ○ None of the above

The value of ______(III) is ______(IV).

Choose the correct answer for (III).

- ○ $\int_0^1 (y^2 - x^2)dy$
- ○ $\int_0^1 x\,dx$
- ○ $\int_0^1 \frac{-2x^3}{3}dx$
- ○ $\int_0^x x\,dy$

Choose the correct answer for (IV).

○ -1/6
○ 1/6
○ 1/2
○ xy

Step (5)

The value of the given doubly integral $\int_0^1\int_0^x (y^2 - x^2)\,dydx$ is.....

Choose the correct answer.

○ 1/6
○ -1/6
○ -1/2
○ 1/2

EXERCISE : 04 Completed

EXERCISE : 05

PROBLEM

Evaluate $\int_0^1\int_{-x}^{\sqrt{x}} \frac{y}{(1-x)}\,dydx$

EVALUATION

Step (1)

Evaluate the innermost integral $\int_{-x}^{\sqrt{x}} \frac{y}{(1-x)}\,dy$

Step (2)

As we are integrating with respect to '*y*', treat the variable '*x*' as constant.

Step (3)

The value of $\int_{-x}^{\sqrt{x}} \frac{y}{(1-x)} dy$ is ....

- ○ $\frac{1}{2}x$
- ○ $\frac{x(1-x)}{2}$
- ○ $\frac{(\sqrt{x}-x)}{2}$
- ○ x

Step (4)

Now, integrate the result _____(I) with respect to _____(II).

Choose the correct answer for (I).

- ○ $\frac{1}{2}x$
- ○ $\frac{x(1-x)}{2}$
- ○ $\frac{(\sqrt{x}-x)}{2}$
- ○ x

Choose the correct answer for (II).

- ○ x
- ○ y
- ○ None of the above

The value of _____(III) is _____(IV).

Choose the correct answer for (III).

- ○ $\int_{-x}^{\sqrt{x}} x dx$
- ○ $\int_{0}^{1} \frac{x}{2} dx$
- ○ $\int_{0}^{1} \frac{x(1-x)}{2}$
- ○ $\int_{0}^{1} \frac{\left(\sqrt{x}-x\right)}{2} dx$

Choose the correct answer for (IV).

- ○ 1
- ○ 1/2
- ○ 1/4

Step (5)

The value of the given integral $\int_{0}^{1}\int_{-x}^{\sqrt{x}} \frac{y}{(1-x)} dydx$ is.....

Choose the correct answer.

- ○ 1
- ○ 1/2
- ○ 1/4
- ○ $1/\sqrt{2}$

EXERCISE : 05 Completed

EXERCISE : 06

PROBLEM

Evaluate $\int_1^3 \int_0^1 (1+4xy)dxdy$

EVALUATION

Step (1)

Evaluate the innermost integral $\int_0^1 (1+4xy)dx$

Step (2)

As we are integrating with respect to – – – (I), treat the variable – – – – (II) as constant.

Choose the correct answer for (I).

- ○ x
- ○ y
- ○ None of the above

Choose the correct answer for (II).

- ○ x
- ○ y
- ○ None of the above

Step (3)

The value of $\int_0^1 (1+4xy)dx$ is ....

Choose the correct answer.

- ○ (1+4x)
- ○ (1+4y)
- ○ (1+2y)
- ○ (1+2x)

Step 4)

Now, integrate the result _____(I) with respect to _____(II).

Choose the correct answer for (I).

- ○ 1+4x
- ○ 1+4y
- ○ 1+2y
- ○ 1+2x

Choose the correct answer for (II).

- ○ x
- ○ y
- ○ None of the above

The value of _____(III) is _____(IV).

Choose the correct answer for (III).

- ○ $\int_1^3 (1+4x)dx$
- ○ $\int_1^3 (1+2x)dy$
- ○ $\int_1^3 (1+4y)dy$
- ○ $\int_1^3 (1+2y)dy$

Choose the correct answer for (IV).

- ○ 10
- ○ 18
- ○ 2(1+2x)
- ○ 6

Step (5)

The value of the given integral $\int_1^3 \int_0^1 (1+4xy)dxdy$ is.....

Choose the correct answer.

- ○ -10
- ○ 10
- ○ 18
- ○ 6

EXERCISE : 06 Completed

EXERCISE : 07

PROBLEM

Evaluate $\int_0^2 \int_1^2 (y - 3x^2)\,dy\,dx$

EVALUATION

Step (1)

Evaluate the integral ....

Choose the correct answer.

- ○ $\int_0^2 (y - 3x^2)\,dy$
- ○ $\int_0^2 (y - 3x^2)\,dx$
- ○ $\int_1^2 (y - 3x^2)\,dy$
- ○ $\int_1^2 (y - 3x^2)\,dx$

Step (2)

As we are integrating with respect to – – –(I), treat the variable – – – –(II) as constant.

Choose the correct answer for (I).

- ○ x
- ○ y
- ○ None of the above

Choose the correct answer for (II).

- ○ x
- ○ y
- ○ None of the above

Step (3)

The value of the integral _____(I) is _____(II).

Choose the correct answer for (I).

- ○ $\int_0^2 (y - 3x^2)dy$
- ○ $\int_0^2 (y - 3x^2)dx$
- ○ $\int_1^2 (y - 3x^2)dx$
- ○ $\int_1^2 (y - 3x^2)dy$

Choose the correct answer for (II).

- ○ $\frac{3}{2} - 3x^2$
- ○ y - 7
- ○ 2y - 8
- ○ $2 - 6x^2$

Step (4)

Now, integrate the result _____(I) with respect to _____(II).

Choose the correct answer for (I).

- ○ $\frac{3}{2} - 3x^2$
- ○ y - 7
- ○ 2y - 8
- ○ 2 - $6x^2$

Choose the correct answer for (II).

- ○ x
- ○ y
- ○ None of the above

The value of _____(III) is _____(IV).

Choose the correct answer for (III).

- ○ $\int_1^2 (2 - 6x^2)dx$
- ○ $\int_1^2 \left(\frac{3}{2} - 3x^2\right)dx$
- ○ $\int_1^2 (y - 7)dx$
- ○ $\int_0^2 (2y - 8)dy$

Choose the correct answer for (IV).

- ○ -5
- ○ -12
- ○ - 11/2
- ○ 12

Step (5)

The value of the given integral $\int_0^2\int_1^2 (y-3x^2)\,dy\,dx$ is.....

Choose the correct answer.

- ○ -5
- ○ -12
- ○ -11/2
- ○ 12

EXERCISE : 07 Completed

I hope that you might have acquired the knowledge of problem solving.

Now for your practice, three problems are given to you.

You solve them and check your answers with the answer of the problems.

EXERCISE : 08

PROBLEM

Evaluate $\int_{-1}^{0}\int_{-1}^{x+1} (xy-x)\,dy\,dx$

EVALUATION

Do you want to verify your answer ?
Press for *Innermost integral value*
Press for *Answer to the given Double Integral* NEXT PROBLEM

EXERCISE : 08 OVER

EXERCISE : 09

PROBLEM

Evaluate $\int_{-1}^{1}\int_{0}^{1}(8-x^2-y^2)\,dx\,dy$

EVALUATION

Do you want to verify your answer ?
Press for *Innermost integral value*
Press for *Answer to the given Double Integral* NEXT PROBLEM

EXERCISE : 09 Over

EXERCISE : 10

PROBLEM

Evaluate $\int_{0}^{1}\int_{-3}^{3}\frac{xy^2}{x^2+1}\,dy\,dx$

EVALUATION

Do you want to verify your answer ?
Press for *Innermost integral value*
Press for *Answer to the given Double Integral*

That's all students !

EXERCISE : 10 Over

CONDUCT OF THE EXPERIMENT

Flow Chart for the Conduct of Experiment

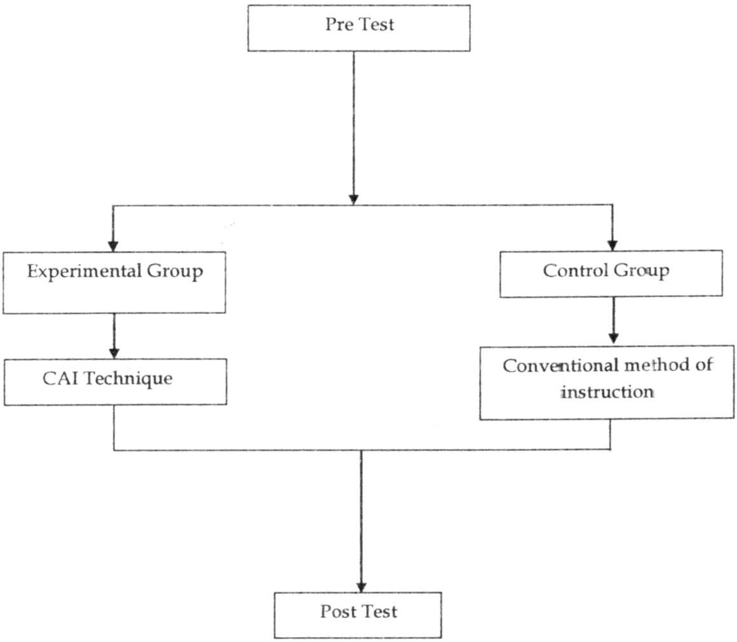

Experimental Design

The following experimental design was adopted for the study.

R =

E_R	P_r	T_1	P_0
C_R	P_r	T_2	P_0

Where, E_R and C_R denote the samples chosen for Experimental group and control group respectively.

P_r - denotes the pre-test measure of the scholastic performance in Double Integrals.

P_0 - denotes the post-test measure of the scholastic performance in Double Integrals.

T_1 - denotes teaching through *CAI*, and

T_2 - denotes teaching through conventional method.

Different strategies were used for teaching the students in the experimental group and control group.

Treatment of the Control Group

As the size of the control group was 114, the investigator divided the group into two of equal size, for the purpose of convenience. The students of control group were subjected to the achievement test (pre-test) constructed by the investigator on the selected units in Double Integrals. The items in the pre test and post test were one and the same, but the order of the items were different.

The control group was then exposed to the conventional lecture–demonstration method using models, diagrams, charts and overhead projector. After the completion of the teaching sessions, the investigator administered the post-test. The medium of instruction was English.

Treatment of the Experimental Group

The experimental group was subjected to the achievement test– (pre-test) constructed by the investigator on the selected units in Double Integrals.

Then the experimental group was exposed through LCD projector, to the handling of mouse, page option, chapter option, hyperlinks, typing of answers to the questions etc. During the *CAI* proper care was taken to clear the doubts and the problem likely to be faced by the students. They were provided with writing materials and permitted to take own time to complete the lesson.

The students were again assessed with the help of same achievement test which was used for pre-test. The medium of instruction was English.

CONCLUSION

The details of the method adopted in the conduct of this quasi-experimental study are furnished in this chapter. The particulars of data analysis are presented in the next chapter.

CHAPTER 5

EFFECT OF *CAI* IN TEACHING AND LEARNING DOUBLE INTEGRALS – AN ANALYSIS

CAI PREFERENCE INDEX-ANALYSIS

In this part of the chapter, an attempt has been made to find out the preference of Computer Assisted Instruction (*CAI*) to Conventional Method of Instruction (CMI). Preference of a person is a state of mind and there is no universally accepted tool to measure the same. At this stage, it is pertinent to explain the methodology adopted to construct this *CAI* preference index.

The students were required to indicate the preference in respect of *CAI* and conventional method of instruction by stating excellent, good, satisfactory or unsatisfactory. For objective analysis, these qualitative grades are converted into quantitative terms. A pilot study was carried out by taking 50 rural and 50 urban students. They were asked to assign points (out of a maximum of 10) for the particular level of preference they indicated for each method. To ensure uniformity a 'forced' distribution of points was adopted for convenience, namely, 8-10 for excellent, 6-8 for good, 4-6 for satisfactory and 0-4 points for unsatisfactory.

These average values when multiplied by the respective 'frequencies' would give the total value of preferences, the same when divided by the total frequency for the respective factor would give the preference index for that factor.

Table 1
Average Values Assigned by Urban Students (Points Out of 10)

	Numerical Values for				
Method of Instruction	*Excellent*	*Good*	*Satis-factory*	*Unsatis-factory*	*Total*
CAI (Computer Assisted Instruction)					
Number of students	38	8	4	–	50
Total value of preferences	366.99	59	20	–	445.99
Average values	9.66	7.38	5	–	8.92
CMI (Conventional Method of Instruction)					
Number of students	6	27	17	–	50
Total value of preferences	48.40	196.20	85	–	329.6
Average values	8.06	7.26	5	–	6.59

Table 2
Average Values Assigned by Rural Students (Points Out of 10)

	Numerical Values for				
Method of Instruction	*Excellent*	*Good*	*Satis-factory*	*Unsatis-factory*	*Total*
CAI (Computer Assisted Instruction)					
Number of students	17	29	4	–	50
Total value of preferences	155.5	213.4	24	–	392.9
Average values	9.15	7.36	6	–	7.86
CMI (Conventional Method of Instruction)					
Number of students	3	19	28	–	50
Total value of preferences	26	139.5	147.2	–	312.7
Average values	8.67	7.34	5.26	–	6.25

The total number of students considered as the sample for this study consists of 70 rural students and 212 urban students. They were asked to give their preferences in respect of Computer Assisted Instruction and Conventional Method of Instruction by stating excellent, good, satisfactory or unsatisfactory. The number of students who indicated the different levels of preferences were multiplied by the average values arrived at, as shown in Table 1 and 2. The preference indices for Computer Assisted Instruction and Conventional method of Instruction were worked out for rural and urban sample students. Arithmetic mean (A.M) and Geometric mean (G.M) were calculated to ascertain the preference indices for different classification of students based on medium of instruction (Tamil and English), secondary school education (Govt. School and Private School) and sex (male and female). The results of the analysis for different classification of the students are shown below:

Table 3
Preference Index Based on Medium of Instruction

	Rural		*Urban*	
Medium of Instruction	*A.M.*	*G.M.*	*A.M.*	*G.M.*
Tamil				
CAI	7.82	7.77	8.33	8.15
CMI	6.17	6.07	6.51	6.39
English				
CAI	7.56	7.49	8.41	8.22
CMI	6.32	6.21	6.78	6.67

As shown in Table 3, the higher values of A.M. and G.M. indicate whether the medium of instruction is Tamil or English, Computer Assisted Instruction is preferred to Conventional Method of Instruction both in the case of students with rural background and urban background.

Table 4
Preference Index based on Schooling

	Rural		*Urban*	
Schooling	*A.M.*	*G.M.*	*A.M.*	*G.M.*
Government				
CAI	7.26	7.22	7.50	7.33
CMI	6.28	6.17	6.51	6.39
Private				
CAI	8.06	8.00	8.47	8.29
CMI	6.18	6.08	6.76	6.65

The preference for Computer Assisted Instruction is amplified as evidenced in Table 4, in the case of students with rural background and urban background. This is found to hold good irrespective of the schooling done by the students viz. whether they have done their schooling in Government institutions or private institutions.

Table 5
Preference Index based on sex

	Rural		*Urban*	
Sex	*A.M.*	*G.M.*	*A.M.*	*G.M.*
Male				
CAI	7.72	7.67	8.01	7.81
CMI	6.19	6.09	6.32	6.20
Female				
CAI	–	–	8.64	8.47
CMI	–	–	6.96	6.87

As indicated in Table 5, the higher values of Arithmetic mean and Geometric mean show whether the students are male or female, Computer Assisted Instruction is preferred to Conventional Method of Instruction both in the case of students with rural background and urban background.

Table 6
Preference Index for the Total Sample Students

	Rural		*Urban*	
Method of Instruction	*A.M.*	*G.M.*	*A.M.*	*G.M.*
CAI	7.72	7.67	8.39	8.21
CMI	6.19	6.09	6.74	6.63

In the case of total number of sample students with rural background and urban background, the preference is towards Computer Assisted Instruction. This is obvious from Table 6 with the higher values of A.M. and G.M. for Computer Assisted Instruction when compared with Conventional Method Instruction.

It may be concluded that all sample students, irrespective of their classification based on medium of instruction, sex and schooling, prefer Computer Assisted Instruction for learning 'Double Integrals'.

ACHIEVEMENT LEVEL - DIFFERENTIAL ANALYSIS

This study was undertaken to analyse the effect of 'CAI' techniques on some selected cognitive and conative variables with respect to teaching of "Double Integrals" in Calculus at undergraduate level. The analysis was made with special reference to the achievement levels. Differential analysis was done for the classification variables sex, locale, language of instruction.

Analysis of the Entry Level Behaviour

In an experimental study, it is necessary to find out the entry level parameter of the groups under study so that if a significant difference is found, suitable modifications can be made in the design of the study and analysis of the data, depending on the outcome of the analysis of the entry level behaviour. Hence, it was necessary to check whether the groups under study could be equated on the entry level parameters.

In the present study, the parameter used was the achievement of undergraduate students in the pre-test on 'Double Integrals'. The details of checking the equivalence of the groups on the entry level parameter is given below:

Table 7
Pre-test Achievement Scores

Group	*Size (N)*	*Mean ($\bar{X}$)*	*S.D.*	*Z - value*
Experimental group	168	12.15	4.14	0.58(NS)
Control group	114	12.46	4.55	

Critical value for 0.05 level = 1.96
NS - Not significant.

The calculated Z-value 0.58 is less than the critical value 1.96 corresponding to the 0.05 level of significance. This implies that the difference in the mean scores under consideration was not significant. Therefore, it is concluded that the experimental group and the control group did not differ significantly in the mean scores at pre-test level.

Analysis of the Terminal Behaviour

In the experimental study, it is also essential to find the significant difference in the achievement level of the two study groups at post–test level.

Table 8
Post-Test Achievement Scores

Group	*Size (N)*	*Mean* ($\bar{X}$)	*S.D.*	*Z - value*
Experimental group	168	25.67	6.68	3.77*
Control group	114	23.09	4.81	

Critical value 0.05 level = 1.96 *Significant at 0.05 level

The calculated Z-value 3.77 is greater than the critical value 1.96 and is significant at 0.05 level. This implies that the difference in mean scores between two groups is significant. Therefore, it is concluded that the achievement of the experimental group was significantly different from the achievement of the control group.

Analysis of Gain Scores

The difference between the mean scores of post-test and pre-test is the achievement gain score. The achievement gain scores of the experimental group and control group are tested in order to find out whether significant difference between them exists or not.

Table 9
Mean Gain Scores Between Experimental and Control Groups

Group	*Size (N)*	*Mean gain Score*	*S.D.*	*Z - value*
Experimental group	168	13.51	6.82	3.54*
Control group	114	10.63	6.64	

Critical Value for 0.05 level = 1.96 *Significant at 0.05 level.

The calculated Z-value 3.54 is greater than the critical value 1.96 corresponding to the 0.05 level of significance. This indicates that the difference in the mean scores under consideration was significant. Therefore, it is concluded that the experimental group and the control group differed significantly.

The above analysis and the higher mean score of the experimental group prove that this group has performed better than the control group. Hence it can emphatically be said that the Computer Assisted Instruction was superior to conventional method of teaching in the achievement of undergraduate students in 'Double Integrals', since these two groups were equal ability groups.

Analysis of Area-wise (Rural and Urban) Achievement

Table 10
Mean Gain Scores between Experimental and Control Groups (Students with Rural Background)

Group	*Size (N)*	*Mean gain Score*	*S.D.*	*Z - value*
Experimental group	36	12.39	5.47	1.65 (NS)
Control group	34	10.00	6.58	

Critical Value for 0.05 level = 1.96 NS = Not Significant

The calculated Z-value 1.65 is less than the critical value 1.96 corresponding to the 0.05 level of significance. This shows that the difference in the mean gain scores between the two groups was not significant. Hence, as far as the rural back ground students are concerned, the gain in the experimental group and the control group students were found to be the same.

Table 11
Mean Gain Scores between Experimental and Control Groups (Students with Urban Background)

Group	*Size (N)*	*Mean gain Score*	*S.D.*	*Z - value*
Experimental group	132	13.82	7.11	3.02*
Control group	80	10.90	6.65	

-Critical Value for 0.05 level = 1.96 * Significant at 0.05 level

The calculated Z-value 3.02 is greater than the critical value 1.96 corresponding to the 0.05 level of significance. This implies that the difference in the mean gain scores between the two groups was significant. The higher mean gain score of the experimental group proves that this group has performed better than the control group. Hence it is concluded that the students with urban background gained more when they were taught 'Double Integrals' through Computer Assisted Instruction than those taught through conventional method.

Analysis of Gender-wise Achievement

Table 12
Mean Gain Scores between Experimental and Control Groups of Male Students

Group	*Size (N)*	*Mean gain Score ($\bar{X}$)*	*S.D.*	*Z - value*
Experimental group	105	14.72	5.98	3.17*
Control group	57	11.23	7.08	

Critical Value for 0.05 level = 1.96 *Significant at 0.05 level

The calculated value 3.17 is greater than the critical value 1.96 corresponding to the 0.05 level of significance. This means that the mean gain scores of the experimental group and the control group differed significantly. The higher mean gain score of the experimental group reveals that 'Double Integrals' taught through *CAI* gave better results than that of conventional method among male students.

Table 13
Mean Gain Scores between Experimental and Control Groups of Female Students

Group	*Size (N)*	*Mean gain Score*	*S.D.*	*Z - value*
Experimental group	63	11.49	7.59	1.16(NS)
Control group	57	10.04	6.12	

Critical Value for 0.05 level = 1.96 NS - Not Significant

The calculated value 1.16 is less than the critical value 1.96 corresponding to 0.05 level of significance. From the above it is evident that the difference in gain between the two groups were not significant. Hence the two groups viz., experimental and control groups gained equally well.

Analysis of Instructional Medium-wise (at Secondary School Level) Achievement

Table 14
Mean Gain Scores between Experimental and Control Groups of Students Studied through Tamil Medium

Group	*Size (N)*	*Mean gain Score*	*S.D.*	*Z - value*
Experimental group	43	11.02	5.16	1.18(NS)
Control group	34	9.24	7.53	

Critical Value for 0.05 level = 1.96 NS = Not Significant

The calculated value 1.18 is less than the critical value 1.96 corresponding to the 0.05 level of significance. This implies that the difference in the mean gain scores between the two groups is not significant. Therefore, it was concluded that the gain of the two groups were observed to be equal.

Table 15
Mean of Gain Scores between Experimental and Control Groups of Students Studied through English Medium

Group	*Size (N)*	*Mean gain Score*	*S.D.*	*Z - value*
Experimental group	125	14.37	7.10	3.36*
Control group	80	11.23	6.13	

Critical Value for 0.05 level = 1.96 * Significant at 0.05 level

The calculated value 3.36 is found to be greater than the critical value 1.96 corresponding to 0.05 level of significance. From the above table, it is obvious that the mean gain scores of the two groups viz. experimental and control groups differed significantly. Hence it is concluded that the students who have studied in English medium at higher secondary level, gained better when they were taught through *CAI*.

Analysis of Gain Scores of Subgroups in the Experimental Group

Analysis of Area-wise (Rural and Urban) Achievement Through CAI

Table 16
Area-wise Comparison of Achievement gain Scores of Students Learnt through *CAI*

Locality	*Size (N)*	*Mean gain Score*	*S.D.*	*Z - value*
Rural	36	12.39	5.47	1.30 (NS)
Urban	132	13.82	7.11	

Critical Value for 0.05 level = 1.96 NS = Not Significant

The calculated Z-value 1.30 is less than the critical value 1.96 corresponding to 0.05 level of significance. This shows that the mean gain scores of students with rural background and urban background did not differ significantly. Hence the gain scores of rural background and urban backg round students were observed to be equal in the experimental group.

Analysis of Gender-wise Achievement Through CAI

Table 17
Gender-wise Comparison of Achievement Gain Scores of Students Learnt Through *CAI*

Sex	*Size (N)*	*Mean gain Score*	*S.D.*	*Z - value*
Male	105	14.72	5.98	2.88*
Female	63	11.49	7.59	

Critical Value for 0.05 level = 1.96 * significant at 0.05 level

The calculated Z-value 2.88 is greater than the critical value 1.96 corresponding to 0.05 level of significance. This shows that the mean gain scores of male and female students differed significantly. From the table, the higher mean gain score of the male students shows that their performance were observed to be better than that of female students when they learnt 'Double Integrals' through Computer Assisted Instruction.

Analysis of Instructional Medium-wise (at Secondary School Level) Achievement Through CAI

Table 18
Instructional Medium-wise (at Secondary School Level) Comparison of Achievement Gain Scores of Students Learnt Through *CAI*

Medium	*Size (N)*	*Mean gain Score*	*S.D.*	*Z - value*
Tamil	43	11.02	5.16	3.31*
English	125	14.37	7.10	

Value for 0.05 level = 1.96 *Significant at 0.05 level

The calculated Z-value 3.31 is greater than the critical value 1.96 corresponding to 0.05 level of significance. Therefore it is concluded that the mean gain scores of the students studied in Tamil medium and English medium differ significantly. The higher mean gain score of the English medium students indicates that their performance was better than the students studied in Tamil medium up to higher secondary level.

Analysis of Achievement Based on Selected Cognitive and Conative Variables

The selected cognitive and conative variables taken for the purpose of analysis in this study are knowledge, understanding, application and skill of the students.

Table 19
Comparison of Mean Gain Scores for Selected Cognitive and Conative Variables

Cognitive or conative variable	*Group*	*N*	*Mean gain scores*	*S.D.*	*Z - Value*
Knowledge	Experimental	168	4.57	3.88	0.59(NS)
	Control	114	4.33	2.84	
Understanding	Experimental	168	3.99	2.77	3.24*
	Control	114	2.84	3.01	
Application	Experimental	168	3.52	2.96	4.25*
	Control	114	2.11	2.59	
Skill	Experimental	168	1.43	2.28	0.28 (NS)
	Control	114	1.35	2.24	

Critical Value for 0.05 level = 1.96 *significant at 0.05 level
NS = Not Significant

From the above table, it is inferred that the mean gain scores of the experimental group and the control group differed significantly at the variables 'understanding' and 'application'. The higher mean scores of the experimental group indicate that their performances based on understanding and application of the concept were better than the control group. Thus as far as the 'understanding' and 'application of the concepts are concerned, the students who learnt 'Double Integrals' through *CAI* performed better than the students who learnt the concept through the conventional instruction.

Table 20
Comparison of Mean Gain Scores for Selected Cognitive and Conative Variables - Students with Rural Background

Cognitive or conative variable	*Group*	*N*	*Mean gain scores*	*S.D.*	*Z - Value*
Knowledge	Experimental	36	4.72	4.69	0.81 (NS)
	Control	34	4.00	2.47	
Understanding	Experimental	36	3.50	2.92	1.93(NS)
	Control	34	2.29	2.28	
Application	Experimental	36	3.78	1.99	2.49*
	Control	34	2.35	2.72	
Skill	Experimental	36	0.39	2.44	1.57 (NS)
	Control	34	1.35	2.69	

Critical Value for 0.05 level = 1.96 *significant at 0.05 level
NS = Not Significant

From the above table, it is inferred that there was significant difference between the experimental group and control group of students at the 'application' of the knowledge. Thus the *CAI* on 'Double Integrals' gave better performance than conventional method of instruction at the application of the learnt concept. In all the remaining three variables viz., 'knowledge', 'understanding' and 'skill', the experimental group and control group performed equally well.

Table 21
Comparison of Mean Gain Scores for Selected Cognitive and Conative Variables – Students with Urban Background

Cognitive or conative variable	*Group*	*N*	*Mean gain scores*	*S.D.*	*Z - Value*
Knowledge	Experimental	132	4.53	3.63	0.12 (NS)
	Control	80	4.48	2.97	
Understanding	Experimental	132	4.12	2.72	2.42*
	Control	80	3.08	3.24	
Application	Experimental	132	3.45	3.17	3.68*
	Control	80	2.00	2.53	
Skill	Experimental	132	1.71	2.15	1.24 (NS)
	Control	80	1.35	2.02	

Critical Value for 0.05 level = 1.96 *Significant at 0.05 level
NS = Not Significant

From the above table, it is inferred that based on the understanding and application of the knowledge, the experimental group differed significantly from control group. Thus the urban based students who learnt 'Double Integrals' through *CAI*, performed better than the students who learnt through conventional method at the understanding and application of the knowledge. The *CAI* and conventional instruction have produced equal performances among the students at the 'knowledge' and 'skill' levels.

Table 22
Comparison of Mean Gain Scores for Selected Cognitive and Conative Variables –Male Students

Cognitive or conative variable	*Group*	*N*	*Mean gain scores*	*S.D.*	*Z - Value*
Knowledge	Experimental	105	5.41	3.66	1.34 (NS)
	Control	57	4.70	2.94	
Understanding	Experimental	105	4.32	2.66	3.65*
	Control	57	2.67	2.81	
Application	Experimental	105	3.77	2.79	4.13*
	Control	57	1.96	2.58	
Skill	Experimental	105	1.22	2.25	1.76 (NS)
	Control	57	1.89	2.38	

Critical Value for 0.05 level = 1.96 *significant at 0.05 level
NS = Not Significant

From the above table, it is inferred that, as far as 'understanding' and 'application' of the concept are concerned, the experimental group differed significantly from the Control group. The higher mean gain scores of the experimental group prove that the male students who learnt 'Double Integrals' through *CAI* performed better than those students who learnt through conventional method at the understanding and application of the knowledge. Also the *CAI* and the conventional method of instruction have produced equal performance among the male students based on the 'Knowledge' and 'Skill' levels.

Table 23
Comparison of Mean Gain Scores for Selected Cognitive and Conative Variables - Female Students

Cognitive or conative variable	*Group*	*N*	*Mean gain scores*	*S.D.*	*Z - Value*
Knowledge	Experimental	63	3.17	3.83	1.32 (NS)
	Control	57	3.96	2.69	
Understanding	Experimental	63	3.43	2.86	0.74 (NS)
	Control	57	3.02	3.18	
Application	Experimental	63	3.11	3.18	1.64 (NS)
	Control	57	2.25	2.60	
Skill	Experimental	63	1.78	2.28	2.51*
	Control	57	0.81	1.94	

Critical Value for 0.05 level = 1.96 *significant at 0.05 level
NS = Not Significant

From the above table, it is inferred that, at the development of skill, the experimental group differed significantly from the control group. Thus the female students who learnt "Double Integrals" through *CAI* acquired better skills than the female students who learnt through conventional instruction. But the performance of the female students based on the remaining variables viz., 'knowledge', 'understanding' and 'application' is found to be equal whether they learnt through *CAI* or conventional method of instruction.

Table 24
Comparison of Mean Gain Scores for Selected Cognitive and Conative Variables – Tamil as Medium of Instruction

Cognitive or conative variable	*Group*	*N*	*Mean gain scores*	*S.D.*	*Z - Value*
Knowledge	Experimental	43	3.81	4.31	0.12 (NS)
	Control	34	3.71	3.60	
Understanding	Experimental	43	2.93	2.42	1.07 (NS)
	Control	34	3.71	3.63	
Application	Experimental	43	3.53	3.19	3.87*
	Control	34	1.35	1.66	
Skill	Experimental	43	0.74	2.28	0.52 (NS)
	Control	34	0.47	2.28	

Critical Value for 0.05 level = 1.96 *significant at 0.05 level
NS = Not Significant

From the above table, it is inferred that the mean gain scores of the experimental group and the control group differed significantly at the 'application' of the concept. The higher mean score of the experimental group shows that the *CAI* produced better performance than the conventional method of instructions at the 'application' of the knowledge acquired among the students whose medium of instructions at secondary level was Tamil. The *CAI* and conventional instruction produced equal performance among the students (whose medium of instruction was Tamil) at the remaining three variables viz., 'knowledge', 'understanding' and 'skill'.

Table 25
Comparison of Mean Gain Scores at Selected Cognitive and Conative Variables – English as Medium of Instruction

Cognitive or conative variable	*Group*	*N*	*Mean gain scores*	*S.D.*	*Z - Value*
Knowledge	Experimental	125	4.83	3.69	0.55 (NS)
	Control	80	4.60	2.40	
Understanding	Experimental	125	4.35	2.80	4.88*
	Control	80	2.48	2.61	
Application	Experimental	125	3.52	2.88	2.68*
	Control	80	2.43	2.84	
Skill	Experimental	125	1.66	2.23	0.20 (NS)
	Control	80	1.73	2.12	

Critical Value for 0.05 level = 1.96 *significant at 0.05 level
NS = Not Significant

From the table given above it is obvious that as far as the 'understanding' and 'application' of the concept are concerned, the experimental groups differed significantly from control groups. The higher mean gain scores of the experimental groups at the 'understanding' and 'application' levels prove that the *CAI* produced better performance than the conventional method of instruction among students whose medium of instruction was English at the secondary level of education. In case of remaining two variables viz., acquisition of 'knowledge', and 'skill', *CAI* and conventional method of instruction produced equal performance among students whose medium of instructions was English.

Analysis of Achievement (Through CAI) of Subgroups Based on Selected Cognative and Conative Variables

From the above table, it is inferred that the mean gain scores of the rural background students and urban background students differed significantly in acquiring skill in "Double Integrals" at 0.05 level of significance. As the mean gain scores of the students with urban back ground was higher than the students with rural back ground students, the *CAI* developed better performance in developing skill in the concept taught.

Table 26
Area-wise (Rural and Urban) Comparison of Mean Gain Scores for Selected Cognitive and Conative Variables - Experimental Group

Cognitive or conative variable	*Group*	*N*	*Mean gain scores*	*S.D.*	*Z - Value*
Knowledge	Rural	36	4.72	4.69	0.23 (NS)
	Urban	132	4.53	3.63	
Understanding	Rural	36	3.50	2.92	1.15 (NS)
	Urban	132	4.12	2.72	
Application	Rural	36	3.78	1.99	0.75 (NS)
	Urban	132	3.45	3.17	
Skill	Rural	36	0.39	2.44	2.96*
	Urban	132	1.71	2.15	

Critical Value for 0.05 level = 1.96 *significant at 0.05 level
NS = Not Significant

Table 27
Gender-wise Comparison of Mean Gain Scores for Selected Cognitive and Conative Variables - Experimental Group

Cognitive or conative variable	*Group*	*N*	*Mean gain scores*	*S.D.*	*Z - Value*
Knowledge	Male	105	5.41	3.66	3.72*
	Female	63	3.17	3.83	
Understanding	Male	105	4.32	2.66	2.01*
	Female	63	3.43	2.86	
Application	Male	105	3.77	2.79	1.36 (NS)
	Female	63	3.11	3.18	
Skill	Male	105	1.22	2.25	1.54 (NS)
	Female	63	1.78	2.28	

Critical Value for 0.05 level = 1.96 *significant at 0.05 level
NS = Not Significant

From the above table, it is inferred that the mean gain scores of male and female students differed significantly at the acquisition of knowledge and understanding. The higher mean scores of the male students proved that the performance of the students with urban background was better than that of students with rural background in learning "Double Integrals" through *CAI* with respect to acquisition of knowledge and understanding. But in the case of other variables viz., 'application' and 'skill', no significant difference was observed and hence it is concluded that both the male and female students performed equally when they were taught "Double Integrals" through *CAI*.

Table 28
Instructional Medium-wise Comparison of Mean Gain Scores for Selected Cognitive and Conative Variables - Experimental Group

Cognitive or conative variable	*Group*	*N*	*Mean gain scores*	*S.D.*	*Z - Value*
Knowledge	Tamil Medium	43	3.81	4.31	1.38 (NS)
	English Medium	125	4.83	3.69	
Understanding	Tamil Medium	43	2.93	2.42	3.19*
	English Medium	125	4.35	2.80	
Application	Tamil Medium	43	3.53	3.19	0.03 (NS)
	English Medium	125	3.52	2.88	
Skill	Tamil Medium	43	0.74	2.28	2.29*
	English Medium	125	1.66	2.23	

Critical Value for 0.05 level = 1.96 *significant at 0.05 level
NS = Not Significant

From the above table, it is inferred that the mean gain scores of the students studied in Tamil Medium and English Medium differed significantly at 'understanding' and acquisition of 'skill' in the concepts. The higher mean gain scores proved that the performance of the students who studied in English Medium is better than the students who studied in Tamil Medium when they learn 'Double Integrals' through *CAI* with respect to 'understanding' and acquisition of 'skill'. No significant difference was observed between students studied in Tamil Medium and English Medium with respect to acquisition of knowledge and application of the concept.

Table 29
Instructional Medium-wise Comparison of Mean Gain Scores of Male Students for Selected Cognitive and Conative Variables - Experimental Group

Cognitive or conative variable	*Group*	*N*	*Mean gain scores*	*S.D.*	*Z - Value*
Knowledge	Tamil Medium	43	3.81	4.31	3.67*
	English Medium	62	6.52	2.61	
Understanding	Tamil Medium	43	2.93	2.42	4.95*
	English Medium	62	5.29	2.39	
Application	Tamil Medium	43	3.53	3.19	0.69 (NS)
	English Medium	62	3.94	2.46	
Skill	Tamil Medium	43	0.74	2.28	1.81 (NS)
	English Medium	62	1.55	2.17	

Critical Value for 0.05 level = 1.96 *significant at 0.05 level
NS = Not Significant

From the above table, it is inferred that the mean gain scores of the male students with Tamil and English as their media of instructions (at secondary school lèvel) differed significantly for the variables acquisition of 'knowledge' and 'understanding' of the concept learnt. For the above two variables the higher mean gain scores of students with English as their medium of instruction at secondary level, indicate that their performance were better than that of Tamil medium students. No significant differences between the mean scores were observed between the above two groups in case of the variables 'application' and acquisition of 'skill'. Thus the performance of the above two groups of students were found to be equal with respect to 'application' and acquisition of 'skill'.

Table 30
Area-wise (Rural and Urban) Comparison of Mean Gain Scores of Male Students for Selected Cognitive and Conative Variables - Experimental Group

Cognitive or conative variable	*Group*	*N*	*Mean gain scores*	*S.D.*	*Z - Value*
Knowledge	Rural	36	4.72	4.69	1.22 (NS)
	Urban	69	5.77	2.92	
Understanding	Rural	36	3.50	2.92	2.21*
	Urban	69	4.75	2.41	
Application	Rural	36	3.78	1.99	0.02 (NS)
	Urban	69	3.77	3.13	
Skill	Rural	36	0.39	2.44	2.67*
	Urban	69	1.65	2.01	

Critical Value for 0.05 level = 1.96 *significant at 0.05 level
NS = Not Significant

From the above table, it is evident that the mean gain scores of male students with rural and urban background differed significantly in case of the variables 'understanding' and development of 'skill'. The higher mean gain scores of the male students with urban background shows that their performance are found to be better than that of male students with rural back ground. For the remaining variables viz., acquisition of 'knowledge' and 'application', no significant differences were observed between their respective mean gain scores of the above two groups of students. Hence their performances were observed to be equal whether the male students belong to rural or urban areas.

Table 31
Gender-wise Comparison of Mean Gain Scores of Students with Urban Background for Selected Cognitive and Conative Variables-Experimental Group

Cognitive or conative variable	*Group*	*N*	*Mean gain scores*	*S.D.*	*Z - Value*
Knowledge	Male	69	5.77	2.92	
	Female	63	3.17	3.83	4.34*
Understanding	Male	69	4.75	2.41	
	Female	63	3.43	2.86	2.86*
Application	Male	69	3.77	3.13	
	Female	63	3.11	3.18	1.19 (NS)
Skill	Male	69	1.65	2.01	
	Female	63	1.78	2.28	0.33 (NS)

Critical Value for 0.05 level = 1.96 *significant at 0.05 level
NS = Not Significant

From the above table, it is inferred that the mean gain scores of the male and female students with urban background differed significantly for the variables acquisition of 'knowledge' and 'understanding'. The higher mean scores of the male students of the above two groups indicate that their performance were found to be better than those of female students with urban back ground. As far as remaining two variables viz. 'application' and acquisition of 'skill' are concerned no significant difference was observed for the above two groups. For the above two variables, the performance were found to be equal among urban students whether they were male or female.

ACHIEVEMENT LEVEL–MULTIPLE REGRESSION ANALYSIS

In this study, an attempt was made to assess the relative importance of various factors influencing achievement level of the students. The search for critical determinants of achievement level was carried out through multivariate analysis using step-wise regression and multiple regression techniques. The purpose of this analysis is to find out answers to the following questions:

(i) Is there a significant relationship between achievement level and variables under study?

(ii) Which combination of independent factors explain maximum variation in achievement level?

(iii) Is there multicollinearity between explanatory factors?

For the purpose of statistical analysis, the dependent variable Y denoted as achievement level was derived from the gain scores obtained by the students. The gain score was obtained by the difference between the achievement scores of the students 'before' and 'after' the Computer Assisted Instruction. This gain score represents the achievement level of the students. The independent variables considered for this purpose are income of the family (X_1), educational level of the father (X_2) educational level of the mother (X_3) and the size of the family (X_4). These informations were collected through questionnaire from the students.

Based on the above factors the following models were constructed and the contribution of each factor in the model was analysed.

Model I: $\hat{Y} = b_{10} + b_{11}X_1 + b_{12}X_2 + b_{13}X_3 + b_{14}X_4 + \epsilon$

Model II: $\hat{Y} = b_{20} + b_{22}X_2 + b_{23}X_3 + b_{24}X_4 + \epsilon$

Model III: $\hat{Y} = b_{30} + b_{32}X_2 + b_{33}X_3 + \epsilon$

Here the error term ϵ is assumed to be normally distributed with N $(0,\sigma^2)$. The parameters in the above models are estimated by the method of least squares, using Gauss-Markov's theorem. By this principle, the best linear unbiased estimator (BLUEs) of b are

$$\hat{b} = (X^1 X)^{-1} X^1 Y \text{ with}$$

$$E(\hat{b}) = b \text{ and } Var(\hat{b}) = \sigma^2 (X^1 X)^{-1}$$

Here $X^1 X$ denote the covariance matrix of explanatory factors X_1, X_2, X_3 and X_4

Using the above techniques the unknown parameters and their standard errors are calculated.

Achievement Level Models

Achievement Level Model I

The estimated model is

$$\hat{Y} = -584.253 + 9.1794\,X_1 + 16.8440\,X_2 - 26.7683X_3 + 102.8711X_4 + \in$$
$$(0.7129) \quad (1.2602) \quad (2.0963) \quad (7.9992)$$

In order to study the variation in achievement levels of different sets of students, Analysis of Variance (ANOVA) techniques are applied and presented from Tables 32 to 36.

Table 32
ANOVA Based on ($Y : X_1, X_2, X_3, X_4$)

Source of variation (SV)	*Degrees of freedom (df)*	*Sum of squares (SS)*	*Mean sum of Squares (MSS)*	*F value*
Due to X_1, X_2, X_3, X_4	4	52.7939	13.1985	67.4425
Residual	7	1.3699	0.1957	
Total	11	54.1638		

The calculated value of F for (4,7) df is 67.4425, which is verified as significant at 5% level of significance.

In order to study the individual contribution of these four factors, step-wise multiple regression techniques are applied and the following conclusions are drawn.

Table 33
ANOVA Based on X_1 Alone in ($Y: X_1, X_2, X_3, X_4$)

SV	*Df*	*SS*	*MSS*	*F value*
Due to X_1 alone	1	7.1874	7.1874	1.5300
Addition of X_2, X_3, X_4	3	45.6065	15.2022	77.6811
Due to X_1, X_2, X_3, X_4	4	52.7939	13.1985	
Residual	7	1.3699	0.1957	
Total	11	54.1638		

For X_1 alone, the calculated value of F is 1.5300 for (1,10) df which is verified as not significant at 5% level of significance. For additional effect of X_2, X_3, X_4 towards Y, the calculated value of F is 77.6811 which is verified as significant at 5% level.

Table 34
ANOVA Based on X_2 alone in ($Y: X_1, X_2, X_3, X_4$)

SV	*df*	*SS*	*MSS*	*F value*
Due to X_2 alone	1	19.7046	19.7046	5.7182
Addition of X_1, X_3, X_4	3	33.0893	11.0298	64.4264
Due to X_1, X_2, X_3, X_4	4	52.7939	13.1985	
Residual	7	1.3699	0.1712	
Total	11	54.1638		

For X_2 alone, the calculated value of F is 5.7182 for (1,10) df, which is verified as significant at 5% level of significance.

For additional effect of X_1, X_3, and X_4 towards Y, the calculated value of F is 64.4264, which is verified as significant at 5% level.

Table 35

ANOVA Based on X_3 Alone in (Y: X_1, X_2, X_3, X_4)

SV	*df*	*SS*	*MSS*	*F value*
Due to X_3 alone	1	17.2850	17.2850	4.6870
Addition of X_1, X_2, X_4	3	35.5089	11.8363	69.1373
Due to X_1, X_2, X_3, X_4	4	52.7939	13.1985	
Residual	7	1.3699	0.1712	
Total	11	54.1638		

For X_3 alone, the calculated value of F is 4.6870 for (1,10) df, which is verified as not significant at 5% level of significance.

For additional effect of X_1, X_2, X_4 towards Y, the calculated value of F is 69.1373, which is verified as significant at 5% level of significance.

Table 36

ANOVA Based on X_4 alone in (Y: X_1, X_2, X_3, X_4)

SV	*df*	*SS*	*MSS*	*F value*
Due to X_4 alone	1	16.4709	16.4709	4.3698
Addition of X_1, X_2, X_3	3	36.3230	12.1077	70.7225
Due to X_1, X_2, X_3, X_4	4	52.7939	13.1985	
Residual	7	1.3699	0.1712	
Total	11	54.1638		

For X_4 alone, the calculated value of F is 4.3698 for (1,10) df, which is verified as not significant at 5% level of significance.

For additional effect of X_1, X_2, X_3 towards Y; the calculated value of F is 70.7225, which is verified as significant at 5% level of significance.

The net effects of b_{ij}'s are tested with the help of student's t-statistic, by framing the suitable null hypothesis that

$$H_0: b_{1j} = 0 \text{ for all } j = 1,2,3,4$$

The test statistic used is

$$t = \frac{\hat{b}_{ij} - b_{ij}(NH)}{\sqrt{\Sigma e_i^2 / (n-k)} \sqrt{a_{ii}}}$$

Where a_{ii} is the appropriate diagonal element in the matrix $(X^1 X)^{-1}$

The values of 't' are presented in 'summary of results'.

In order to verify the 'multicollinearity' among explanatory factors, the correlation matrix, based on the determinants: ($Y: X_1, X_2, X_3, X_4$) is calculated.

Table 37
Correlation Matrix Based on ($Y: X_1, X_2, X_3, X_4$)

	Y	X_1	X_2	X_3	X_4
Y	1.0000				
X_1	0.3643	1.0000			
	(1.2370)				
X_2	0.6032*	0.4342	1.0000		
	(2.3916)	(1.5242)			
X_3	0.5649	0.7273*	0.8745*	1.0000	
	(2.1649)	(3.3511)	(5.70158)		
X_4	0.5514	0.4080	0.8074*	0.9010*	1.0000
	(2.0901)	(1.4132)	(4.3275)	(6.5677)	

Note: values in the parentheses are corresponding t-values.
*significant at 5% level.

$$\text{Here } t = \frac{r\sqrt{n-2}}{\sqrt{1-r^2}}$$

This statistic follows t – distribution at (n-2) df.

From the above table, it is evident that the factors X_3 and X_4 are multicollinear, since r (X_3 X_4.) = 0.9010.

The multiple correlation coefficient (R^2) and adjusted multiple correlation coefficient $\bar{R}^2$are calculated by using the relation

$$R^2 = \frac{Y^1Y - e^1e}{Y^1Y}$$

where $\hat{e}_i = \hat{Y}_i - \hat{b}_{10} - \hat{b}_{11} X_{1i} - \hat{b}_{12} X_{2i} - \hat{b}_{13} X_{3i} - \hat{b}_{14} X_{4i}$ for i = 1,2,..........12 and $\bar{R}^2 = \left[1-(1-R^2)(n-1)/(n-k\right]$

Table 38

Summary of Results - Achievement Level Model I

Ordinary Regression coefficients	$\hat{\beta}_{11}$ =*0.4931*	$\hat{\beta}_{12}$ =*1.8244*	$\hat{\beta}_{13}$ =*0 8921*	$\hat{\beta}_{14}$ =*6.6252*
L.S. estimators	$\hat{b}_{11}$ =9.1794	$\hat{b}_{12}$ =16.8440	$\hat{b}_{13}$ = -26.7683	$\hat{b}_{14}$ = 102.3714
S.E's ($\hat{b}_{ij}$)	0.7129	1.2602	2.0963	7.9992
t-values	12.8754	13.3657	12.7695	12.8602
F-values	1.5300	5.7182 *	4.6870	4.3698
Multiple correlation coefficient			R^2 = 0.9747*	
Adjusted multiple correlation coefficient			$\bar{R}^2$ = 0.9602*	
Existence of multicollinearity :			X_3 and X_4 are multicollinear.	

* significant at 5% level.

The following inferences are drawn from the above table:

(i) The multiple correlation coefficient between Y: X_1,X_2,X_3,X_4 is $R^2 = 0.9747$.

This implies that these four factors together have 97.47% influence on Y.

(ii) It is verified that $\sum e_i = 0$ and $\sum e^2_i = 1.3860$, is minimum.

This shows that the least square estimates are reliable and can be used for future predictions.

(iii) There is multicollinearity between the factors X_3 and X_4.

Achievement Level Model II

Neglecting the insignificant contribution of X_1 towards Y, the estimated achievement model is

$$\hat{Y} = -12.5349 + 1.3568\, X_2 + 0.0189\, X_3 + 2.1444\, X_4 + \in$$
$$(1.7493) \quad (1.2391) \quad (7.7697)$$

Table 39
ANOVA based on (Y: X_2, X_3, X_4)

SV	*df*	*SS*	*MSS*	*F value*
Due to X_2, X_3, X_4	3	20.3521	6.7840	1.6051
Residual	8	33.8117	4.2265	
Total	11	54.1638		

The calculated value of F for (3,8) df is 1.6051, which is verified as not significant at 5% level of significance.

Table 40.
ANOVA Based on X_2 Alone in (Y: X_2, X_3, X_4)

SV	*df*	*SS*	*MSS*	*F value*
Due to X_2 alone	1	19.7046	19.7046	5.7182
Addition of X_3, X_4	2	0.6475	0.3238	13.0528
Due to X_2, X_3, X_4	3	20.3521	6.7840	
Residual	8	33.8817	4.2265	
Total	11	54.1638		

For X_2 alone, the calculated value of F is 5.7182 for (1,10) df which is verified as significant at 5% level of significance.

For additional effect of X_3 and X_4 towards Y, the calculated value of F is 13.0528 for (8,2) df, which is verified as not significant at 5% level of significance.

Table 41
ANOVA Based on X_3 Alone in (Y: X_2, X_3, X_4)

SV	*df*	*SS*	*MSS*	*F value*
Due to X_3 alone	1	17.2850	17.2850	4.6870
Addition of X_2, X_4	2	3.0671	1.5336	2.7559
Due to X_2, X_3, X_4	3	20.3521	6.7840	
Residual	8	33.8817	4.2265	
Total	11	54.1638		

For X_3 alone the calculated value of F is 4.6870 for (1,10) df, which is verified as not significant at 5% level of significance.

For additional effect of X_2, X_4 towards Y, the calculated value of F is 2.7559, which is verified as not significant at 5% level.

Table 42
ANOVA Based on X_4 Alone in ($Y: X_2, X_3, X_4$)

SV	*df*	*SS*	*MSS*	*F value*
Due to X_4 alone	1	16.4709	16.4709	4.3698
Addition of X_2, X_3	2	3.8812	1.9406	2.1779
Due to X_2, X_3, X_4	3	20.3521	6.7840	
Residual	8	33.8817	4.2265	
Total	11	54.1638		

For X_4 alone, the calculated value of F is 4.3698 for (1,10) df which is verified as not significant at 5% level of significance.

For additional effect of X_2, X_3 towards Y, the calculated value of F is 2.1779, which is verified as not significant at 5% level.

Table 43
Summary of Results-Achievement Level Model II

Ordinary Regression coefficients	$\hat{\beta}_{22}$ =1.8244	$\hat{\beta}_{23}$ =0.8921	$\hat{\beta}_{24}$ =6.6252
L.S. estimators	$\hat{b}_{22}$ =1.3583	$\hat{b}_{23}$ =0.0171	$\hat{b}_{24}$ =2.1522
S.E's ($\hat{b}_{ij}$)	1.7493	1.2391	7.7697
t-values	0.7765	0.0138	0.2770
F-values	5.7182 *	4.6870	4.3698
Multiple correlation coefficient		R^2 = 0.3758	
Adjusted multiple correlation coefficient		$\overline{R}^2$ = 0.1417	

* significant at 5% level.

From the above table, the conclusion drawn is:

The multiple correlation co-efficient between $Y: X_2, X_3, X_4$ is R^2 = 0.3758. This implies that these three factors together have 37.58 % influence on Y.

Achievement Level Model III

Neglecting the insignificant contribution of X_4 towards Y, the estimated model based on determinants ($Y : X_2, X_3$) is

$$\hat{Y} = -3.5491 + \underset{(1.6499)}{1.4031}\, X_2 + \underset{(0.8613)}{0.2515}\, X_3 + \epsilon$$

Table 44
ANOVA Based on (Y: X_2, X_3)

SV	*df*	*SS*	*MSS*	*F value*
Due to X_2, X_3	2	20.0279	10.0140	
Residual	9	34.1359	3.7929	2.6402
Total	11	54.1638		

The calculated value of F for (2,9) df is 2.6402, which is verified as not significant at 5% level of significance.

Table 45
ANOVA Based on X_2 Alone in (Y: X_2, X_3)

SV	*df*	*SS*	*MSS*	*F value*
Due to X_2 alone	1	19.7046	19.7046	5.7182
Addition of X_3	1	0.3233	0.3233	11.7318
Due to X_2, X_3	2	20.0279	10.0140	
Residual	9	34.1359	3.7929	
Total	11	54.1638		

For X_2 alone, the calculated value of F is 5.7182 for (1,10) df which is verified as significant at 5% level of significance.

For additional effect of X_3 towards Y, the calculated value of F is 11.7318 , which is verified as not significant at 5% level.

Table 46
ANOVA Based on X_3 Alone in (Y: X_2, X_3)

SV	*df*	*SS*	*MSS*	*F value*
Due to X_3 alone	1	17.2850	17.2850	4.6870
Addition of X_2	1	2.7429	2.7429	1.3828
Due to X_2, X_3	2	20.0279	10.0140	
Residual	9	34.1359	3.7929	
Total	11	54.1638		

For X_3 alone, the calculated value of F is 4.6870 for (1,10) df which is verified as not significant at 5% level of significance.

For additional effect of X_2 towards Y, the calculated value of F is 1.3828 , which is verified as not significant at 5% level of significance.

Table 47
Summary of Results – Achievement Level Model III

Ordinary Regression coefficients	$\hat{\beta}_{32}$ =*1.8244*	$\hat{\beta}_{33}$ =*0.8921*
L.S. estimators	$\hat{b}_{32}$ =1.4031	$\hat{b}_{33}$ =0.2515
S.E's ($\hat{b}_{ij}$)	1.6499	0.8613
t-values	0.8504	0.2920
F-values	5.7182*	4.6870
Multiple correlation coefficient	R^2 = 0.3698	
Adjusted multiple correlation coefficient	R^2 = 0.2298	

* significant at 5% level.

From the above table the conclusion drawn is : The multiple correlation coefficient between Y : X_2 X_3 is R^2 = 0.3698. This implies that these two factors together have 36.98% influence on Y.

Components of Achievement Level Models

The components of achievement level of the experimental group of this study are acquisition of knowledge, understanding of the concept, application of knowledge and developing the skill. In this study each of these components of achievement level is taken as dependent variable and its relationship with the independent variables viz., income of the family (X_1), educational level of the father (X_2), educational level of the mother (X_3) and the size of the family (X_4) is studied using step-wise regression and multiple regression techniques.

Achievement Level Models Based on Acquisition of Knowledge

The following three models are constructed and unknown parameters are estimated by using Least Square Techniques.

Model I: $\hat{Y} = b_{10} + b_{11}X_1 + b_{12}X_2 + b_{13}X_3 + b_{14}X_4 + \in$

Model II: $\hat{Y} = b_{20} + b_{21}X_1 + b_{22}X_2 + b_{23}X_3 + \in$

Model III: $\hat{Y} = b_{30} + b_{31}X_1 + b_{33}X_3 + \in$

Achievement Level Based on Acquisition of Knowledge – Model I

The estimated model is

$$\hat{Y} = -331.8758 + 5.5999\ X_1 + 9.0391\ X_2 - 15.3002\ X_3 + 58.4138\ X_4 + \in$$
$$(0.4029) \quad (0.7122) \quad (1.1853) \quad (4.5206)$$

Table 48

ANOVA Based on ($Y{:}X_1, X_2, X_3, X_4$)

SV	*df*	*SS*	*MSS*	*F value*
Due to X_1, X_2, X_3, X_4	4	18.3507	4.5877	73.4032
Residual	7	0.4374	0.0625	
Total	11	18.7881		

The calculated value of F for (4,7) df is 73.4032, which is verified as significant at 5% level of significance.

Table 49

Correlation Matrix based on ($Y: X_1, X_2, X_3, X_4$)

	Y	X_1	X_2	X_3	X_4
Y	1.0000				
X_1	0.6308*	1.0000			
	(2.5708)				
X_2	0.4033	0.4342	1.0000		
	(1.3937)	(1.5242)			
X_3	0.5324	0.7273*	0.8745*	1.0000	
	(1.9889)	(3.3511)	(5.7016)		
X_4	0.3947	0.4080	0.8074*	0.9010*	1.0000
	(1.3584)	(1.4132)	(4.3275)	(6.5677)	

Note: values in the parentheses are corresponding t-values.
*significant at 5% level.

From the above table, it is clear that the factors X_3 and X_4 are multi collinear, since r (X_3, X_4) = 0.9010.

Table 50

Summary of Results – Achievement Level Based on Acquisition of Knowledge – Model I

Ordinary Regression coefficients	$\hat{\beta}_{11}=0.5029$	$\hat{\beta}_{12}=0.7185$	$\hat{\beta}_{13}=0.4951$	$\hat{\beta}_{14}=2.7927$
L.S. estimators	$\hat{b}_{11}=5.5999$	$\hat{b}_{12}=9.0391$	$\hat{b}_{13}=-15.3002$	$\hat{b}_{14}=58.4138$
S.E's ($\hat{b}_{ij}$)	0.4029	0.7122	1.1853	4.5206
t-values	13.8991	12.6919	12.9082	12.9218
F-values	6.6081*	1.9428	3.9555	1.8451

Multiple correlation coefficient	$R^2 = 0.9767$*
Adjusted multiple correlation coefficient	$\overline{R}^2 = 0.9634$*
Existence of multicollinearity :	X_3 and X_4 are multicollinear.

*significant at 5% level.

From the above table, the conclusions drawn are:

(i) The Multiple Correlation co-efficient between Y: X_1, X_2, X_3, X_4 is $R^2 = 0.9767$. This implies that these four factors together have 97.67% of influence on Y.

(ii) It is verified that $\sum e_i = 0$ and $\sum e_i^2 = 0.4345$ is minimum. This shows that the least square estimates are reliable and can be used for future predictions.

(iii) There is multicollinearity between the factors X_3 and X_4.

Achievement Level Based on Acquisition of Knowledge Model II

Neglecting the insignificant contribution of X_4 towards Y, the estimated model is

$$\hat{Y} = -4.1032 + 0.5088\, X_1 + 0.5035\, X_2 - 0.1664\, X_3 + \in$$
$$(0.3927) \quad (1.2417) \quad (0.8507)$$

Table 51

ANOVA Based on (Y:X_1,X_2, X_3)

SV	*df*	*SS*	*MSS*	*F value*
Due to X_1, X_2, X_3	3	7.9153	2.6384	1.9413
Residual	8	10.8728	1.3591	
Total	11	18.7881		

The calculated value of F for (3,8) df is 1.9413, which is verified as not significant at 5% level of significance.

Table 52

Summary of Results - Achievement Level Based on Acquisition of Knowledge - Model II

Ordinary Regression coefficients	$\hat{\beta}_{21}$ = *0.5029*	$\hat{\beta}_{22}$ = *0.7185*	$\hat{\beta}_{23}$ = *0.4951*
L.S. estimators	$\hat{b}_{21}$ = 0.5088	$\hat{b}_{22}$ = 0.5035	$\hat{b}_{23}$ = -0.1664
S.E's ($\hat{b}_{ij}$)	0.3927	1.2417	0.8507
t-values	1.2955	0.4055	0.1956
F-values	6.6081*	1.9428	3.9555
Multiple correlation coefficient		R^2 = 0.4213	
Adjusted multiple correlation coefficient		$\bar{R}^2$ = 0.2043	

* significant at 5% level.

From the above Table, The Multiple Correlation co-efficient between Y: X_1, X_2, X_3 is $R^2 = 0.4213$. This implies that these three factors X_1, X_2, X_3 together have 42.13% influence on Y.

Achievement Level based on Acquisition of Knowledge Model III

Neglecting the insignificant contribution of X_2 towards Y, the estimated model is

$$\hat{Y} = -0.2676 + 0.4123\,X_1 + 0.1454\,X_3 + \epsilon$$
$$(0.2975) \quad (0.3471)$$

Table 53
ANOVA Based on (Y:X_1, X_3)

SV	*df*	*SS*	*MSS*	*F value*
Due to X_1, X_3	2	7.6918	3.8459	
Residual	9	11.0963	1.2329	3.1194
Total	11	18.7881		

The calculated value of F is 3.1194, for (2,9) df, which is verified as not significant at 5% level of significance.

Table 54
Summary of Results – Achievement Level Based on Acquisition of Knowledge–Model III

Ordinary Regression coefficients	$\hat{\beta}_{31} = 0.5029$	$\hat{\beta}_{33} = 0.4951$
L.S. estimators	$\hat{b}_{31} = 0.4123$	$\hat{b}_{32} = 0.1454$
S.E's ($\hat{b}_{ij}$)	0.2975	0.3471
t-values	1.3858	0.4189
F-values	6.6081*	3.9555
Multiple correlation coefficient	$R^2 = 0.4094$	
Adjusted multiple correlation coefficient	$\bar{R}^2 = 0.2782$	

* significant at 5% level.

From the above study, the Multiple Correlation co-efficient between Y: X_1, X_3 is $R^2 = 0.4094$. This implies that the factors family income (X_1) and Mother Education (X_3) together have 40.94% influence on Y.

Achievement Level Models Based on Understanding of the Concept

The following three models are estimated by considering the dependent variable as achievement level based on understanding of the concept (Y).

Model I: $\hat{Y} = b_{10} + b_{11}X_1 + b_{12}X_2 + b_{13}X_3 + b_{14}X_4 + \in$

Model II: $\hat{Y} = b_{20} + b_{22}X_2 + b_{23}X_3 + b_{24}X_4 + \in$

Model III: $\hat{Y} = b_{30} + b_{32}X_2 + b_{34}X_4 + \in$

Achievement Level Based on the Understanding of the Concept-Model I

The estimated model is

$$\hat{Y} = -190.6464 + \underset{(0.2156)}{2.8905}\, X_1 + \underset{(0.3811)}{5.6838}\, X_2 - \underset{(0.6343)}{8.6777}\, X_3 + \underset{(2.4192)}{33.1985}\, X_4 + \in$$

Table 55

ANOVA Based on ($Y{:}X_1, X_2, X_3, X_4$)

SV	*df*	*SS*	*MSS*	*F value*
Due to X_1, X_2, X_3, X_4	4	6.3181	1.5795	88.2402
Residual	7	0.1251	0.0179	
Total	11	6.4432		

The calculated value of F for (4,7) df is 88.2402, which is verified as significant at 5% level of significance.

Table 56

Correlation Matrix Based on ($Y{:}\ X_1, X_2, X_3, X_4$)

	Y	X_1	X_2	X_3	X_4
Y	1.0000				
X_1	0.2380 (0.7749)	1.0000			
X_2	0.6724* (2.8727)	0.4342 (1.5242)	1.0000		
X_3	0.5527 (2.0972)	0.7273* (3.3511)	0.8745* (5.7016)	1.0000	
X_4	0.5804* (2.2539)	0.4080 (1.4132)	0.8074* (4.3275)	0.9010* (6.5677)	1.0000

Note: values in the parentheses are corresponding t-values.
* significant at 5% level.

From the above table, it is clear that two factors X_3 and X_4 are multicollinear, since r $(X_3, X_4) = 0.9010$.

Table 57
Summary of Results–Achievement Level Based on Understanding of the Concept–Model I

Ordinary Regression coefficients	$\hat{\beta}_{11} = 0.1111$	$\hat{\beta}_{12} = 0.7015$	$\hat{\beta}_{13} = 0.3010$	$\hat{\beta}_{14} = 2.4050$
L.S. estimators	$\hat{b}_{11} = 2.8905$	$\hat{b}_{12} = 5.6838$	$\hat{b}_{13} = -8.6777$	$\hat{b}_{14} = 33.1985$
S.E's ($\hat{b}_{ij}$)	0.2156	0.3811	0.6343	2.4192
t-values	13.4058	14.9126	13.6800	13.7227
F-values	0.6003	8.2527*	4.3985	5.0796*
Multiple correlation coefficient			$R^2 = 0.9806$*	
Adjusted multiple correlation coefficient			$\bar{R}^2 = 0.9695$*	
Existence of multicollinearity :			X_3 and X_4 are multicollinear.	

* significant at 5% level.

From the above table, the conclusions drawn are:

(i) The Multiple correlation coefficient between $Y{:}X_1,X_2,X_3,X_4$ is $R^2=0.9806$. This implies that these four factors together have 98.06% influence on Y.

(ii) It is verified that $\Sigma e_i = 0$ and $\Sigma e_i^2 = 0.1250$ is minimum. This shows that the least square estimates are reliable and can be used for future predictions.

(iii) There is multicollinearity between the factors X_3 and X_4.

Achievement Level Based on the Understanding of the Concept– Model II

Neglecting the insignificant contribution of X_1 towards Y, the estimated model is

$$\hat{Y} = -10.6295 + \underset{(0.5500)}{0.8074\, X_2} - \underset{(0.3906)}{0.2432\, X_3} + \underset{(2.4431)}{1.4827\, X_4} + \epsilon$$

Table 58
ANOVA Based on (Y: X_2, X_3, X_4)

SV	*df*	*SS*	*MSS*	*F value*
Due to X_2, X_3, X_4	3	3.1012	1.0337	2.4742
Residual	8	3.3420	0.4178	
Total	11	6.4432		

The calculated value of F for (3,8) df is 2.4742, which is verified as not significant at 5% level of significance.

Table 59
Summary of Results–Achievement Level Based on Understanding of the Concept–Model II

Ordinary Regression coefficients	$\hat{\beta}_{22} = 0.7015$	$\hat{\beta}_{23} = 0.3010$	$\hat{\beta}_{24} = 2.4050$
L.S. estimators	$\hat{b}_{22} = 0.8074$	$\hat{b}_{23} = -0.2432$	$\hat{b}_{24} = 1.4827$
S.E's ($\hat{b}_{ij}$)	0.5500	0.3906	2.4431
t-values	1.4680	0.6227	0.6069
F-values	8.2527*	4.3985	5.0796*
Multiple correlation coefficient		$R^2 = 0.4813$	
Adjusted multiple correlation coefficient		$\overline{R}^2 = 0.2868$	

* significant at 5% level.

From the above table, the Multiple Correlation co-efficient between Y: $X_2 X_3 X_4$ is $R^2 = 0.4813$. This implies that these three factors together have 48.13 % influence on Y.

Achievement Level Based on the Understanding of Concept Model III

Neglecting the insignificant contribution of X_3 towards Y, the estimated model is

$$\hat{Y} = -4.9721 + \underset{(0.4346)}{0.6108\, X_2} + \underset{(1.7265)}{0.4463\, X_4} + \epsilon$$

Table 60
ANOVA Based on (Y: X_2, X_4)

SV	*df*	*SS*	*MSS*	*F value*
Due to X_2, X_4	2	2.9392	1.4696	3.7750
Residual	9	3.5040	0.3893	
Total	11	6.4432		

The calculated value of F for (2,9) df is 3.7750, which is verified as not significant at 5% level of significance.

Table 61
Summary of Results–Achievement Level Based on Understanding of the Concept–Model III

Ordinary Regression coefficients	$\hat{\beta}_{32} = 0.7015$	$\hat{\beta}_{34} = 2.4050$
L.S. estimators	$\hat{b}_{32} = 0.6108$	$\hat{b}_{34} = 0.4463$
S.E's ($\hat{b}_{ij}$)	0.4346	1.7265
t-values	1.4054	0.2585
F-values	8.2527*	5.0796*
Multiple correlation coefficient	$R^2 = 0.4562$	
Adjusted multiple correlation coefficient	$\bar{R}^2 = 0.3354$	

* significant at 5% level.

From the above table, the multiple correlation coefficient between Y: X_2 X_4 is $R^2 = 0.4562$. This implies that these two factors together have 45.62% influence on Y.

Achievement Level Models Based on Application of the Knowledge

The following three models are estimated by considering the dependent variable as achievement level based on application of the knowledge (Y).

The models based on the factors (Y: X_1,X_2,X_3,X_4) studied are:

Model I : $\hat{Y} = b_{10} + b_{11}X_1 + b_{12}X_2 + b_{13}X_3 + b_{14}X_4 + \epsilon$

Model II: $\hat{Y} = b_{20} + b_{21}X_1 + b_{22}X_2 + b_{23}X_3 + \epsilon$

Model III: $\hat{Y} = b_{30} + b_{32}X_2 + b_{33}X_3 + \epsilon$

Achievement Level Based on Application of the Knowledge Model-I

The estimated model is:

$$\hat{Y} = \underset{}{49.2301} - \underset{(0.2972)}{0.6823\,X_1} + \underset{(0.5253)}{1.0652\,X_2} + \underset{(0.8742)}{2.1649X_3} - \underset{(3.3342)}{8.5222\,X_4} + \epsilon$$

Table 62
ANOVA Based on (Y:X_1,X_2,X_3,X_4)

SV	*df*	*SS*	*MSS*	*F value*
Due to X_1, X_2, X_3, X_4	4	0.8436	0.2109	6.2030
Residual	7	0.2380	0.0340	
Total	11	1.0816		

The calculated value of F for (4,7) df is 6.2030, which is verified as significant at 5% level of significance.

Table 63
Correlation matrix based on ($Y: X_1, X_2, X_3, X_4$)

	Y	X_1	X_2	X_3	X_4
Y	1.0000				
X_1	0.6588*	1.0000			
	(2.7692)				
X_2	0.6901*	0.4342	1.0000		
	(3.0154)	(1.5242)			
X_3	0.7056*	0.7273*	0.8745*	1.0000	
	(3.1489)	(3.3511)	(5.7016)		
X_4	0.2546	0.4080	0.8074*	0.9010*	1.0000
	(0.8326)	(1.4132)	(4.3275)	(6.5677)	

Note: values in the parentheses are corresponding t-values.
* significant at 5% level.

From the above table, it is clear that two factors X_3 and X_4 are multicollinear, since r (X_3, X_4) = 0.9010

Table 64
Summary of Results–Achievement Level Based on Application of the Knowledge-Model I

Ordinary Regression coefficients	$\hat{\beta}_{11} = 0.0686$	$\hat{\beta}_{12} = 0.1667$	$\hat{\beta}_{13} = 0.0905$	$\hat{\beta}_{14} = 0.4322$
L.S. estimators	$\hat{b}_{11} = -0.6823$	$\hat{b}_{12} = 1.0652$	$\hat{b}_{13} = 2.1649$	$\hat{b}_{14} = -8.5222$
S.E's ($\hat{b}_{ij}$)	0.2972	0.5253	0.8742	3.3342
t-values	2.2961	2.0278	2.4763	2.5560
F-values	10.6255*	15.5577	19.2324*	3.4998
Multiple correlation coefficient			R^2 = 0.4050	
Adjusted multiple correlation coefficient			$\bar{R}^2$ = 0.0650	
Existence of multicollinearity :	X_3 and X_4 are multicollinear.			

* significant at 5% level.

From the above table, following conclusions are drawn:

(i) The multiple correlation coefficient between ($Y: X_1\ X_2\ X_3\ X_4$) is R^2 = 0.4050. This implies that these four factors together have 40.50% influence on Y.

(ii) It is verified that $\sum e_i = 0$ and $\sum e^2_i = 0.6435$, is minimum. This shows that the Least Square estimates are reliable and can be used for future predictions.

(iii) There is multicollinearity between the factors X_3 and X_4

Achievement Level Based on the Application of the Knowledge-Model II

Neglecting the insignificant contribution of X_2 towards Y, the estimated model is :

$$\hat{Y} = 1.4099 + \underset{(0.0683)}{0.6005}\, X_1 + \underset{(0.2159)}{0.1801}\, X_2 - \underset{(0.1479)}{0.0430}\, X_3 + \in$$

Table 65

ANOVA Based on $(Y{:}X_1, X_2, X_3)$

SV	*df*	*SS*	*MSS*	*F value*
Due to X_1, X_2, X_3	3	0.7528	0.2509	6.1050
Residual	8	0.3288	0.0411	
Total	11	1.0816		

The calculated value of F for (3,8) df is 6.1050, which is verified as significant at 5% level of significance.

Table 66

Summery of Results-Achievement Level Based on Application of the Knowledge-Model II

Ordinary Regression coefficients	$\hat{\beta}_{21} = 0.0686$	$\hat{\beta}_{22} = 0.1667$	$\hat{\beta}_{23} = 0.0905$
L.S. estimators	$\hat{b}_{21} = 0.0604$	$\hat{b}_{22} = 0.1801$	$\hat{b}_{23} = -0.0430$
S.E's ($\hat{b}_{ij}$)	0.0683	0.2159	0.1479
t-values	0.8843	0.8343	0.2907
F-values	10.6255*	15.5577*	19.2324*
Multiple correlation coefficient		$R^2 = 0.1996$	

* significant at 5% level.

From the above table, the conclusion drawn is:

The multiple correlation coefficient between $(Y{:}\ X_1\ X_2\ X_3)$ is $R^2 = 0.1996$. This implies that these three factors together have 19.96% influence on Y.

Achievement Level Based on the Application of Knowledge-Model III

Neglecting the insignificant contribution of X_4 towards Y; the estimated model is :

$$\hat{Y} = 2.3922 + \underset{(0.2677)}{0.0643}\,X_2 + \underset{(0.1397)}{0.0611}\,X_3 + \epsilon$$

Table 67
ANOVA Based on (Y:X_2, X_3)

SV	*df*	*SS*	*MSS*	*F value*
Due to X_2, X_3	2	0.1837	0.0919	1.0866
Residual	9	0.8979	0.0998	
Total	11	1.0816		

The calculated value of F for (9,2) df is 1.0866, which is verified as not significant at 5% level of significance.

Table 68
Summary of Results–Achievement Level Based on the Application of Knowledge–Model III

Ordinary Regression coefficients	$\hat{\beta}_{32}$ = *0.1667*	$\hat{\beta}_{33}$ = *0.0905*
L.S. estimators	$\hat{b}_{32}$ = 0.0643	$\hat{b}_{33}$ = 0.0611
S.E's ($\hat{b}_{ij}$)	0.2677	0.1397
t-values	0.2402	0.4373
F-values	15.5577*	19.2324*
Multiple correlation coefficient	R^2 = 0.1697	

* significant at 5% level.

From the above table, the conclusion drawn is:

The Multiple Correlation co-efficient between Y: X_2,X_3 is $R^2 = 0.1697$. This implies that these two factors together have 16.97% influence on Y.

Achievement Level Models Based on Development of the Skills

The following three models are estimated by considering the dependent variable as achievement level based on development of the skills (Y).

Model I: $\hat{Y} = b_{10} + b_{11}X_1 + b_{12}X_2 + b_{13}X_3 + b_{14}X_4 + \in$

Model II: $\hat{Y} = b_{20} + b_{22}X_2 + b_{23}X_3 + b_{24}X_4 + \in$

Model III: $\hat{Y} = b_{30} + b_{32}X_2 + b_{34}X_4 + \in$

Achievement Level Based on the Development of the Skill-Model I

The estimated model is

$$\hat{Y} = -12.9363 - \underset{(0.0483)}{0.0897}\,X_1 + \underset{(0.0855)}{0.3812}\,X_2 - \underset{(0.1422)}{0.1110}\,X_3 + \underset{(0.5425)}{2.2373}\,X_4 + \in$$

Table 69
ANOVA Based on ($Y{:}X_1\ X_2\ X_3\ X_4$)

SV	*df*	*SS*	*MSS*	*F value*
Due to X_1, X_2, X_3, X_4	4	2.6091	0.6523	724.778
Residual	7	0.0066	0.0009	
Total	11	2.6157		

The calculated value of F for (4,7) df is 724.7778, which is verified as highly significant at 5% level of significance.

Table 70
Correlation Matrix Based on ($Y{:}\ X_1, X_2, X_3, X_4$)

	Y	X_1	X_2	X_3	X_4
Y	1.0000				
X_1	0.0608	1.0000			
	(0.1925)				
X_2	0.8472*	0.4342	1.0000		
	(5.0427)	(1.5242)			
X_3	0.7261	0.7273*	0.8745*	1.0000	
	(3.3394)	(3.3511)	(5.7016)		
X_4	0.8994*	0.4080	0.8074*	0.9010*	1.0000
	(6.5065)	(1.4132)	(4.3275)	(6.5677)	

Note: values in the parentheses are corresponding t-values.
* significant at 5% level.

From the above table, it is clear that two factors X_3 and X_4 are multicollinear, since r (X_3, X_4) = 0.9010.

Table 71
Summary of Results - Achievement Level Based on Development of Skills - Model I

Ordinary Regression coefficients	$\hat{\beta}_{11} = 0.0181$	$\hat{\beta}_{12} = 0.5631$	$\hat{\beta}_{13} = 0.2520$	$\hat{\beta}_{14} = 2.3745$
L.S. estimators	$\hat{b}_{11} = -0.0897$	$\hat{b}_{12} = 0.3812$	$\hat{b}_{13} = -0.1110$	$\hat{b}_{14} = 2.2373$
S.E's ($\hat{b}_{ij}$)	0.0483	0.0855	0.1422	0.5425
t-values	1.8553	4.4604	0.7804	4.1243
F-values	0.0372	25.4287*	11.1489*	42.3140*
Multiple correlation coefficient			$R^2 = 0.9975$*	
Adjusted multiple correlation coefficient			$\bar{R}^2 = 0.9961$*	
Existence of multicollinearity :			X_3 and X_4 are multicollinear.	

* significant at 5% level.

From the above table, the conclusions drawn are:

(i) The multiple correlation coefficient between Y: X_1 X_2 X_3 X_4 is $R^2 = 0.9975$. This implies that these four factors together have 99.75 % influence on Y.

(ii) It is verified that $\sum e_i = 0$ and $\sum e_i^2 = 0.0064$ is minimum. This shows that the least square estimates are reliable and can be used for future predictions.

(iii) There is multicollinearity between the factors X_3 and X_4.

Achievement Level Based on the Development of the Skill - Model II

Neglecting the insignificant contribution of X_1 towards Y, the estimated model is

$$\hat{Y} = -18.5215 + \underset{(0.0295)}{0.5325\, X_2} - \underset{(0.0209)}{0.3726\, X_3} + \underset{(0.1309)}{3.2213\, X_4} + \epsilon$$

Table 72
ANOVA Based on (Y: X_2 X_3 X_4)

SV	*df*	*SS*	*MSS*	*F value*
Due to X_1, X_2, X_3, X_4	3	2.6061	0.8687	723.9167
Residual	8	0.0096	0.0012	
Total	11	2.6157		

The calculated value of F for (3,8) df is 723.9167, which is verified as highly significant at 5% level of significance.

Table 73
Summary of Results–Achievement Level Based on Development of Skill–Model II

Ordinary Regression coefficients	$\hat{\beta}_{22} = 0.5631$	$\hat{\beta}_{23} = 0.2520$	$\hat{\beta}_{24} = 2.3745$
L.S. estimators	$\hat{b}_{22} = 0.5325$	$\hat{b}_{23} = -0.3726$	$\hat{b}_{24} = 3.2213$
S.E's ($\hat{b}_{ij}$)	0.0295	0.0209	0.1309
t-values	18.0659	17.8011	24.6022
F-values	25.4287*	11.1489*	42.314*
Multiple correlation coefficient		$R^2 = 0.9964$*	
Adjusted multiple correlation coefficient		$\bar{R}^2 = 0.9951$*	

* significant at 5% level.

From the above table, the conclusion drawn is:

The multiple correlation coefficient between ($Y : X_2, X_3, X_4$) is $R^2 = 0.9964$. This implies that these three factors together have 99.64% influence on Y.

Achievement Level Based on the Development of the Skill-Model III

Neglecting the insignificant contribution of X_3 towards Y, the estimated model is:

$$\hat{Y} = -9.8521 + \underset{(0.1449)}{0.2312\, X_2} + \underset{(0.5757)}{1.6331\, X_4} + \epsilon$$

Table 74
ANOVA Based on ($Y: X_2\ X_4$)

SV	*df*	*SS*	*MSS*	*F value*
Due to X_2, X_4	2	2.2258	1.1129	25.7021
Residual	9	0.3899	0.0433	
Total	11	2.6157		

The calculated value of F for (2,9) df is 25.7021, which is verified as significant at 5% level of significance.

Table 75
Summary of Results–Achievement Level Based on Development of Skill–Model III

Ordinary Regression coefficients	$\hat{\beta}_{32} = 0.5631$	$\hat{\beta}_{34} = 2.3745$
L.S. estimators	$\hat{b}_{32} = 0.2312$	$\hat{b}_{34} = 1.6331$
S.E's ($\hat{b}_{ij}$)	0.1449	0.5757
t-values	1.5951	2.8367
F-values	25.4287*	42.314*
Multiple correlation coefficient	$R^2 = 0.8510$*	
Adjusted multiple correlation coefficient	$\overline{R}^2 = 0.8179$*	

* significant at 5% level.

From the above table, the conclusion drawn is:

The multiple correlation co-efficient between ($Y: X_2\ X_4$) is $R^2 = 0.8510$. This implies that these two factors together have 85.10 % influence on Y.

Table 76
Ranking of Factors Influencing Achievement Level

Study / *Factor Studied*	*Total Achievement*	*Knowledge*	*Under-standing*	*Application*	*Skill*
X1 : Family Income	IV	(I)	IV	III	IV
X2 : Father's Education	(I)	III	(I)	(II)	(II)
X3 : Mother's Education	(II)	(II)	III	(I)	III
X4 : Family Size	III	IV	(II)	IV	(I)

Considering the ranks obtained in the total achievement of the students, achievement level based on acquisition of knowledge, understanding of the concept, application of knowledge and development of skill, father's education primarily influences the achievement level of the students when they learn 'Double integrals' through *CAI*. The secondary influence on the achievement level is mother's education. On the whole, parental education influences the achievement level of the students to a great extent.

WORKING RESULTS OF THE HYPOTHESES

The hypotheses stated in the first chapter were tested on the basis of the data presented and analysed in this chapter. The working results of the hypotheses are as follows:

Hypotheses Accepted

1. Undergraduate students who were taught 'Double Integrals' through *CAI* and conventional instruction methods differ significantly in their post-test achievement scores. (vide Table 8)
2. Undergraduate students learning 'Double Integrals' through *CAI* and conventional instruction methods differ significantly in their achievement. (vide Table 9)
3. Undergraduate students with urban background learning 'Double Integrals' through *CAI* and conventional instruction methods differ significantly in their achievement. (vide Table 11)
4. Undergraduate male students, learning 'Double Integrals' through *CAI* and conventional instruction methods differ significantly in their achievement. (vide Table 12)
5. Undergraduate students who were taught English medium (at their secondary school level), learning 'Double Integrals' through *CAI* and conventional instruction methods differ significantly in their achievement. (vide Table 15)
6. In learning 'Double Integrals' through *CAI* at undergraduate level, male students differ significantly from female students in their achievement. (vide Table 17)
7. In learning 'Double Integrals' through *CAI* at undergraduate level, students studied in Tamil medium and English medium at secondary school level differ significantly in their achievement (vide Table 18)
8. Undergraduate students learning 'Double Integrals' through *CAI* and conventional instruction methods differ significantly in their

   (i) understanding and (ii) application (vide Table 19)

9. Undergraduate students with rural background, learning 'Double Integrals' through *CAI* and conventional instruction methods differ significantly in their "application". (vide Table 20)

10. Undergraduate students with urban background, learning 'Double Integrals' through *CAI* and conventional instruction methods differ significantly in their

    (i) understanding and (ii) application (vide Table 21)

11. Undergraduate male students, learning 'Double Integrals' through *CAI* and conventional instruction methods differ significantly in their

    (i) understanding and (ii) application (vide Table 22)

12. Undergraduate female students, learning 'Double Integrals' through *CAI* and conventional instruction methods differ significantly in their "skill". (vide Table 23)

13. Undergraduate students, who studied in Tamil medium (at their secondary school level), learning 'Double Integrals' through *CAI* and conventional methods differ in their "application". (vide Table 24)

14. Undergraduate students, who studied in English medium (at their secondary school level), learning 'Double Integrals' through *CAI* and conventional methods differ in their

    (i) understanding and (ii) application (vide Table 25)

15. In learning 'Double Integrals' through *CAI* at undergraduate level, students with rural background differ significantly from the students with urban background in their "skill". (vide Table 26)

16. In learning, 'Double Integrals' through *CAI* at undergraduate level, male students differ significantly from female students in their

    (i) knowledge and (ii) understanding (vide Table 27)

17. In learning 'Double Integrals' through *CAI* at undergraduate level, students who studied in Tamil

medium differ significantly from the students who studied in English medium (at their secondary school level) in their

(i) understanding and (ii) skill (vide Table 28)

18. Parental education influences the achievement of the learners, when they learn 'Double Integrals' through *CAI*.

Hypotheses Rejected

1. Undergraduate students, with rural background learning 'Double Integrals' through *CAI* and through conventional instruction method differ significantly in their achievement. (vide Table 10)
2. Undergraduate female students, learning 'Double Integrals' through *CAI* and conventional instruction methods differ significantly in their achievement. (vide Table 13)
3. Undergraduate students, who were taught in Tamil medium (at their secondary school level), learning conventional 'Double Integral' through *CAI* and instruction methods differ in their achievement. (vide Table 14)
4. In learning 'Double Integrals' through *CAI* at undergraduate level, students with rural background differ significantly from the students with urban background in their achievement (vide Table 16)
5. Undergraduate students learning 'Double Integrals' through *CAI* and conventional instruction methods differ significantly in their
   (i) knowledge and (ii) skill (vide Table 19)
6. Undergraduate students with rural background learning 'Double Integrals' through *CAI* and conventional instruction methods differ significantly in their
   (i) knowledge and (ii) understanding and (iii) skill
   (vide Table 20)
7. Undergraduate students with urban background learning 'Double Integrals' through *CAI* and conventional instruction methods differ significantly in their

(i) knowledge and (ii) skill (vide Table 21)

8. Undergraduate male students, learning 'Double Integrals' through *CAI* and conventional instruction methods differ significantly in their
(i) knowledge and (ii) skill (vide Table 22)

9. Undergraduate female students, learning 'Double Integrals' through *CAI* and conventional instruction methods differ significantly in their
(i) knowledge (ii) understanding and (iii) application (vide Table 23)

10. Undergraduate students, who studied in Tamil medium (at their secondary school level), learning 'Double Integrals' through *CAI* and conventional instruction methods differ in their
(i) knowledge (ii) understanding and (iii) skill (vide Table 24)

11. Undergraduate students, who studied in English medium (at their secondary school level), learning 'Double Integrals' through *CAI* and conventional instruction methods differ in their (i) knowledge and (ii) skill (vide Table 25)

12. In learning 'Double Integrals' through *CAI* at undergraduate level, students with rural background differ significantly from the students with urban background in their
(i) knowledge (ii) understanding and (iii) application (vide Table 26)

13. In learning 'Double Integrals' through *CAI* at undergraduate level, male students differ significantly from female students in their
(i) application and (ii) skill (vide Table 27)

14. In learning 'Double Integrals' through *CAI* at undergraduate level, students who studied in Tamil medium differ significantly from the students who studied in English medium (at their secondary school level) in their
(i) knowledge and (ii) application (vide Table 28)

CHAPTER 6

FINDINGS AND SUGGESTIONS

This chapter gives an account of the summary of findings and conclusions based on the preceding chapters. Scope for the future study and suggestions have also been given at the end of this chapter.

FINDINGS

Computer Assisted Instruction (*CAI*) in our country is still in the infant stage, though the contribution of individual excellence to the field of IT is substantial and remarkable in the recent years. It is hoped that the conclusion of the study would add strength to the existing body of knowledge in teaching and learning of mathematics in general and 'Double Integrals' in particular through *CAI*. The findings based on the analysis made in the preceding chapters are summarized as follows:

1. The objectives are to find out the relationship between the variables taken for the investigation namely, *CAI* and conventional method of instruction in teaching – learning Double Integrals and to study the achievement of students of first year UG courses who have mathematics as their major or as allied subject.
2. Experimental design was adopted to find out the effect of *CAI* on learning 'Double Integrals' by the under-graduate students.

3. An interactive *CAI* package was developed in order to measure the effectiveness of the Computer Assisted Instruction against the conventional method of instruction in 'Double Integrals'.
4. Softwares used for developing the *CAI* package were : Java Script, Java Applet, HTML 4.0, Corel Draw 9.0, 3D Studio Max, Photo Shop 7.0, Flash 5.0, Corel Image Ready, AUTO CAD 2000, Front Page 2000, MS Word and Xara Webstyle.
5. *CAI* package on 'Double Integrals' was administered to the respondents in the experimental group.
6. The effect of *CAI* in Teaching and Learning Double Integrals was analysed using the appropriate statistical tools.

CAI Preference Index Analysis

7. In learning 'Double Integrals', the undergraduate students prefer the Computer Assisted Instruction (*CAI*) rather than the conventional method of instruction, irrespective of their classification based on area (rural or urban), sex (male or female) medium of instruction (Tamil or English) and schooling (Private or Government).

Achievement Level Differential Analysis

8. The achievement of the undergraduate students, taught through *CAI*, is better than the achievement of the students taught through conventional method in 'Double Integrals'.*CAI* is found to be more effective on learners' achievement than conventional method of teaching 'Double Integrals'.
9. For the undergraduate students with urban background, the *CAI* has more positive effect on achievement than the conventional method of teaching 'Double Integrals'.
10. For the undergraduate students whose medium of instruction at the secondary school was English, the

CAI is found to be more effective than the conventional method in learning 'Double Integrals'.

11. For the undergraduate male students, in learning 'Double Integrals' the *CAI* is more effective than the conventional method of teaching.
12. In learning 'Double Integrals' at the undergraduate level, the *CAI* and conventional instruction produce same gain effect in the students with rural background, female students and students whose medium of instruction at their secondary school was Tamil.
13. The undergraduate male students perform better than the female students when they learn 'Double Integrals' though *CAI*. The effectiveness of *CAI* is more on the male students.
14. In learning 'Double Integrals' through *CAI*, the performance of undergraduate students whose medium of instruction at their secondary school was English is better than that of the students whose medium of instruction at their secondary school was Tamil. The effectiveness of *CAI* is more on the students who had English medium at their secondary school level.
15. In learning 'Double Integrals' through *CAI* the performance of the male students whose medium of instruction at their secondary school was English is better than that of the male students whose medium of instruction at their secondary school was Tamil. The *CAI* has more positive effect on the male students who had English medium.
16. In learning 'Double Integrals' through *CAI* at the undergraduate level, the male students with urban background perform better than the female students with the same background. The *CAI* is more effective in the case of male students with urban background.

17. As far as the gain in achievement is concerned, the effectiveness of the *CAI* is same for students with rural background and students with urban background. In learning 'Double Integrals' at undergraduate level, the *CAI* has same effect on both groups of students with rural as well as urban background.
18. In learning 'Double Integrals' at the undergraduate level, the *CAI* is more effective in the realization of instructional objectives viz., 'understanding' and 'application' than the conventional method of teaching.
19. For the undergraduate students with rural background, the *CAI* is more effective, in the realization of the instructional objective viz., 'application' than in the conventional method of teaching 'Double Integrals'.
20. For the undergraduate students with urban background, the *CAI* has more positive effects on the realizations of the instructional objectives viz., 'understanding' and 'application'.
21. For the undergraduate male students, the *CAI* is more effective in the realization of the instructional objectives viz., 'understanding' and 'application'.
22. For the undergraduate female students, the *CAI* is more effective in the realization of the instructional objective viz., 'skill'.
23. For the undergraduate students whose medium of instruction at their secondary level was Tamil, the *CAI* is more effective in the realization of the instructional objective viz., 'application'.
24. For the undergraduate students whose medium of instruction at their secondary level was English, the *CAI* is more effective in the realization of the instructional objectives viz., 'understanding' and 'application'.

25. In learning 'Double Integrals' at the undergraduate level, the *CAI* and the conventional instruction have the same effect in acquiring knowledge and in the case of development of 'skill', the effect was the same for all groups except female students.
26. In *CAI* on 'Double Integrals' at undergraduate level, the students with urban background perform better than the students with rural background in the realization of instructional objective viz., 'skill'. The *CAI* on 'Double Integrals' is more effective on the students with urban background than the students with rural background with respect to the development of skill at the undergraduate level.
27. In learning "Double Integrals' through *CAI* at the undergraduate level, the male students, whose medium of instruction at their secondary school was English, perform better than male students whose medium of instruction at their secondary school was Tamil, in the realization of instructional objectives viz., 'knowledge' and 'understanding'.

    The *CAI* on "Double Integrals' at the undergraduate level, is more effective for the male students who have studied in English medium at secondary school with respect to the acquisition of 'knowledge' and 'understanding' of the concept.
28. In learning 'Double Integrals' through *CAI* at the undergraduate level, the performance of the students, whose medium of instruction at secondary level was English, is better than that of the students whose medium of instruction was Tamil at secondary level, in realizing the instructional objectives viz., 'understanding' and 'skill'.

The *CAI* on 'Double Integrals' has more positive effects on the students who studied their secondary school in English medium with respect to 'understanding' and development of 'skills'.

29. In learning "Double Integrals' through *CAI* at the undergraduate level, the male students with urban background perform better than the male students with rural background in the realization of the instructional objectives viz., 'understanding' and 'skill'.

    The *CAI* on "Double Integrals' at the undergraduate level is more effective in the case of male students with urban background with respect to 'understanding' of concept and development of 'skills'.

30. In learning "Double Integrals' through *CAI* at the undergraduate level, the male students with urban background perform better than female students with urban background in the realization of the instructional objectives viz., 'knowledge' and 'understanding'.

    The *CAI* on "Double Integrals' at the undergraduate level is more effective for the male students with urban background with respect to the acquisition of 'knowledge' and 'understanding' of the concept.

31. As far as the instructional objective 'application' is concerned, the *CAI* on 'Double Integrals' has the same effect on the undergraduate students, irrespective of their classification based on area (rural or urban) sex and medium of instruction.

Achievement Level - Multiple Regression Analysis

32. In the study of the total achievement level of the students, it is observed that the four explanatory

factors such as income of the family, educational level of the father, educational level of the mother and size of the family together contribute to the extent of 97.47% when the learning of 'Double Integrals' takes place through *CAI*.

33. Based on the individual contribution of each variable, father's education and mother's education rank first and second respectively in the total achievement of the students when they learn 'Double Integrals' through *CAI*.

34. The achievement level of the students based on the acquisition of knowledge in learning 'Double Integrals' through *CAI* is determined by the four variables (income of the family, education of father, education of mother and size of the family) to the extent of 97.67%.

35. Family income and mother's education are ranked first and second respectively in the achievement level of the students based on acquisition of knowledge when they learn 'Double Integrals' through *CAI*.

36. The achievement level of the students based on the understanding of the concept in learning 'Double Integrals' through *CAI* is determined by the four variables to the extent of 98.06%.

37. Father's education and family size are ranked first and second respectively in the achievement level of the students based on understanding of the concept when they learn 'Double Integrals' through *CAI*.

38. The achievement level of the students based on the application of the knowledge in learning 'Double Integrals' through *CAI* is determined by the four variables to the extent of 40.5%.

39. Mother's education and Father's education are ranked first and second respectively in the

achievement level of the students based on application of the knowledge when they learn 'Double Integrals' through *CAI*.

40. The achievement level of the students based on the development of skill in the learning 'Double Integrals' through *CAI* is determined by the four variables to the extent of 99.75%.
41. Family size and Father's education are ranked first and second respectively in the achievement level of the students based on development of skills when they learn 'Double Integrals' through *CAI*.
42. Considering the ranks obtained in the total achievement of the students, the achievement level based on acquisition of knowledge, understanding of the concept, application of knowledge and development of the skill, father's education primarily influences the students when they learn 'Double Integrals' through *CAI*. The secondary influence on the achievement level is mother's education. On the whole, parental education influences the achievement level of the students to a great extent.

CONCLUSIONS

Generally the students prefer *CAI* to the conventional method of instruction. However, all the topics of mathematics cannot be taught through *CAI*. But whenever and wherever possible, conventional method of instruction may be replaced or supplemented by *CAI*. For teaching 'Double Integrals' *CAI* is an effective method of instruction. *CAI* helps to increase the achievement level of the students. In terms of acquisition of knowledge and skill development, the effect of *CAI* on achievement does not differ from conventional method of instruction. For understanding the concept and application of knowledge, *CAI* is helpful to increase the achievement level of the students when compared with conventional method of instruction.

As experienced by the researcher, the use of mathetics programming techniques, under programmed learning has helped the learners in effective application of the knowledge. Besides parental education influences the achievement level of the students to a great extent when they learn 'Double Integrals' through *CAI*.

SCOPE FOR FURTHER STUDY

The researcher has identified the following research gaps based on his experience in this study which will throw light on areas for the future researchers in education to pursue their research work in higher education.

1. The effectiveness of *CAI* can be studied on different branches of mathematics both at the undergraduate and post graduate levels.
2. The effectiveness of software packages which provide drill and practice on different branches of mathematics can be studied.
3. *CAI* packages with concept mapping technique can be developed on various branches of mathematics and their effectiveness can be studied.
4. Computerised test administration packages on several branches of mathematics can be developed and their effectiveness can be studied.
5. *CAI* packages for under-achievers can be developed on all branches of mathematics and their effectiveness can be studied.
6. *CAI* packages for gifted students can be developed on various branches of mathematics and their effectiveness can be studied.
7. Simulation packages can be developed for laboratory-oriented subjects like Physics, Chemistry, Botany, Zoology etc. and their effectiveness can be studied.
8. The speed of learning can be studied with respect to the variables like sex, socio-economic backgrounds, medium of instruction etc.

9. *CAI* packages can be developed for other disciplines like Commerce, Economics, Management Studies etc., and their effectiveness can be studied.
10. The effectiveness of learning through internet can be studied.

SUGGESTIONS

The researcher has made the following suggestions which will help the Policy-makers, Institutional agencies, Academicians and Researchers in Higher Education to enhance the quality of Education:

1. While framing the curriculum in mathematics, the authorities of the universities may identify the appropriate areas where computers can be used for teaching.
2. For the identified areas in the mathematics curriculum, self - learning *CAI* packages may be developed and distributed to the affiliated institutions.
3. Good teachers are generally unaware of the capabilities of the computer, while good computer professionals do not usually understand the foundations of good instructions. Developing computer based instruction requires knowledge of both. Therefore a subject on the development of *CAI* may be included at the post-graduate curriculum of various disciplines.
4. Tests are crucial part of the instructional process. The content has to be relevant to the instruction it follows, or must meet the goals of the test. The questions must cover all objectives thoroughly and the validity of the test should not be compromised because of perceived time constraints. Computerized Test Administration System may be implemented in all disciplines in general and mathematics in particular.
5. Distance learning programmes can be made effective through *CAI* packages.

6. In each and every educational institution, an Electronic Library may be maintained by collecting *CAI* packages for several disciplines.
7. Simulation packages can be made available for lab-oriented subjects for conducting practicals in the educational institutions.
8. University Grants Commission may come forward to encourage the researchers and Institutions of Higher Education by providing adequate financial and technical support for the development of *CAI* packages in all spheres of higher education.

BIBLIOGRAPHY

Aggarwal, Y.P., Statistical Methods–Concepts, Applications and Computation, Sterling Publishers Private Limited, 1988.

Akker, J.V.D., Keursten, Paul and Plomp, Tjeerd, The Integration of Computer Use in Education., *International Journal of Educational Research,* Volume 17, No. 1, 1992.

Alessi, Stephen, M., and Trollip, Stanley, R., Computer Based Instruction - Methods and Development, Prentice - Hall, Inc., Englewood cliffs, New Jersey, 1985.

Alison B. Boss., Technology Reviews, U.S.A. 1985.

Anderson, R. C., "How to Construct Achievement Tests to Assess Comprehension", Review of Educational Research, 43 (1972), 145–170.

Anderson, R.C. & Faust, G.W. Educational Psychology: The Science of Instruction and Learning, New York, Dodd, Mead, 1973.

Ann Barron, Designing Web-based Training, *British Journal of Education,* Vol. 29, No. 4, 1994.

Baker, Philip and Yeater, Harry, Introducing Computer Assisted Learning, Prentice Hall International, 1985.

Barren, D.W., Crowford, R.F., Farrow, P.F., Garratt, P.W. and Hall, W., Women and the Micro Computer Science, Southampton University, 1985.

Berk, R.A. (Ed.), Criterion-referenced Measurement: The State of the Art, Baltimore, MD: The Johns Hopkins University Press, 1981.

Berk, R.A. (Ed.), Educational Evaluation Methodology: The State of the Art. Baltimore, MD: The Johns Hopkins University Press, 1981.

Berkey, Dennis, D. and Blanchard, Paul, Calculus, Saunders College Publishing, Harcourt Brace Jovanovich College Publishers, 2000.

Best, John.W and Kahn, James V., Research in Education, Prentice - Hall of India, New Delhi, 2000.

Bjarnason, L. D., Strategies for Improving the Mathematics Course (Alberta), University of Alberta (Canada), 1995.

Bloom, B.S., & Hastings, J.T. & Madaus, G. F., Handbook on Formative and Summative Evaluation of Student Learning, New York: McGraw-Hill, 1991.

Bohn, M. J., A Comparison of Achievement between Students Taking a Developmental Mathematics Course Using Computer-Assisted Instructions and Students Taking the Course in the Traditional Classroom Setting, University of Houston, 1994.

Brehler, R., Report on the ICME Symposium on the Influence of Computers and Informatics on Mathematics and its Teaching, Reprinted in ICME bulletin, June 1987.

Briggs, L. J. (Ed.), Instructional Design: Principles and Applications. Englewood Cliffs, NJ: Educational Technology Publications, 1987.

Burkhard, H., and Davis, L. D., Debate on the Micro Computer: Miracle or Menace to the Mathematical Education, Proceedings of the Fifth International Congress on Mathematics Education, Boston, 1986.

Burton, B. S., The Effect of Computer Assisted Instruction and Other Selected Variables on the Academic Performance of Adult Students in Mathematics and Reading, Grabling State University, 1995.

Callisson, W. L., Using Computers in the Class-room, Prentice Hall Inc., New Jercy, U.S.A, 1988.

Carl B. Boyer, A History of Mathematics, John Wiley and Sons Inc, 1968.

Carnine, D. & Silbert, J., Direct Instruction Reading. Columbus, OH: Chas E. Merrill, 1979.

Chen, Li-Ling, Effects of Static Graphics, Animated Graphics and Digital Video on Students' Performance and Attitude in Computer Assisted Instruction, Ph.D Thesis, The University of Texas, Austin, 1995.

Clark, R. E. "Reconsidering Research on Learning from Media", *Review of Educational Research,* 53 (1983), 445-59.

Collins, Thomas, Jr., The Effects of Computer Assisted Algebra Instruction on Achievement, Mathematics Anxiety Levels and Attitudes Toward Personal use of Computers of Students in an Historically Black University, Ph.D thesis, University of South Florida, 1996.

Cooley, W.W. & Lohnes, P. R. Evaluation Research in Education, New York: Irvington Publishers, 1987.

Cox, Janet Karen, The effects of Contextual Learning-Based Instruction Versus Computer Assisted Instruction on Basic Skills in Selected Vocational Courses, Oklahoma State University, 1996.

Cox, Margaret, J., The Computer in the Science Curriculum, *International Journal of Educational Research*, Volume 17, No. 1, 1992.

Dwyer, F. M. Strategies for Improving Visual Learning. State College, PA: Learning Services, 1988.

Edwin Christmann and John Badgett, A Comparative Analysis of the Effects of Computer Assisted Instruction on Student Achievement in Differing Science and Demographical Areas, 1999.

Engelmann, S. Direct Instruction. Englewood Cliffs, NJ: Educational Technology Publications, 1980.

Engelmann, S. & Carnine, D. Theory of Instruction: Principles and Applications, New York: Irvington, 1982.

Erickson, G. and Erickson, L., Females and Science Achievement, Evidence, Explanations and Implications, *Science Education*, 63, No. 2, 63-69, 1984.

Fionnuala Flanagan, Mathematics an Educational Enquiry into the Use of Concept Mapping and Multimedia, to Enhance the Understanding of Mathematics, Dublin City University, June 2002.

Fleming, M. & Levie, W.H., Instructional Message Design: Principles from the Behavioural Science, Englewood Cliffs, NJ: Educational Technology Publications, 1978.

Fletcher Debbe, Reviewing for High-Stakes Test Preparation in Mathematics, 2001.

Fredenberg, Virgil Grant, Supplemental Visual Computer-Assisted Instruction and Student Achievement in Freshman College Calculus (Visualization), Montana State University, 1993.

French, Dorothy M., A Comparison Study of Computer Assisted Instruction Using Interactive Software versus Traditional Instruction in a College Pre-calculus Course, Temple University, 1997.

Gagne, R. M. & Briggs, L. J. Principles of Instructional Design, New York, Holt, Rinehart & Winston, 1979.

Gittinger, D.J., Co-operative Learning and Computer Assisted Instruction : A Comparison of Student Achievement in Arithmetic and Algebra in the College Developmental Algebra Class, The University of Texas at Austin, 1994.

Gronlund, N. E., Measurement and Evaluation in Teaching, New York: Macmilan, 1981.

Harding, Girls and Science and Technology (GASAT), The School Science Review, Australia, January 1982.

Hawkins, The Science Education of Girls, Longman for Schools Commission, Australia, January 1986.

Heines, J. M., Screen Design Strategies for Computer-Assisted Instruction. Bedford, MA: Digital Press, 1984.

Howson, A. G., and Kahane, J. P., The Influence of Computers and Informatics on Mathematics and its Teaching, Proceedings of International Symposium Held at Strasbury, Cambridge University Press, England, 1987.

International Council for Computers in Education. Evaluator's Guide for Microcomputer-based Instructional Packages. Eugene: ICCE, University of Oregon, 1982.

Issa, Raja, R.A., The Effects of Multi-media-based Safety Training, University of Florida, 1998.

Jackson, D. N. & Messick, S. (Ed.), Problems in Human Assessment. New York: McGraw-Hill, 1987.

Jamsa, Kris, Suleiman "Sam" lalani, Steve Weakley., Frank Bros & Co., New Delhi, 1997.

Jayathilakan, V., Concept Mapping as a Strategy for Teaching Zoology at Higher Secondary level, unpublished Ph.D thesis, Bharathidasan University, Tiruchy, 1992.

Jones, N.B., & Vaughan, L., Evaluation of Educational Software : A Guide to Guides, Austin, TX: Southwest Educational Development Laboratory and Northeast Regional Exchange, 1983.

Joy F.Xin, Integrating Technology in Instruction in an Inclusive Classroom for Diverse, Rowan University, 2000.

Julian C. Stanley and Kenneth D. Hopkins, Educational and Psychological Measurement and Evaluation, Prentice - Hall of India Private Limited, New Delhi, 1978.

Johnston. J., Econometric Methods, McGraw-Hill Kogakusha, Ltd. Tokyo, 1980.

Kapur J.N., Support Needed for Education and Research in Mathematical Sciences, The Mathematics Students No. 33, 1990.

Kapur, J. N., Mathematical Education at the Cross Roads, Mathematical Education, October - December, 1988.

Kapur, J. N., The Impact of Computers and Informatics on Mathematical Education and Research Mathematics Education, January-March, 1987.

Kay Judy, Collins, P., Lubin, J., Poiner, G., Prosser, M., Bishop, R. and Watson, K., Investigation of the Status of Women at Early Stages of Professionally Accredited Tertiary Computer Science and Data Processing Programs and Learning, University of Sydney, Australia, 1986.

Kay, Judy and Micheal Prosser, A Formative Study of the First Programming Module of Computer Science, The University of Sydney, Australia, 1983.

Kernighan, B. and Plauger, P. Elements of Programming Style. New York: Mc Graw-Hill, 1988.

Kernighan, B., & Plauger, P. Software Tools. Reading, M.A: Addison-Wesley, 1986.

Khandare, S.S., Programming in Java, S.Chand and Company, New Delhi, 2002.

Knotos, G., Computer Education, 1985.

Konavalina, John, Lorry Stephans and Stanly William, *Australian Educationist Journal*, 1983.

Koutsoyiannis. A., Theory of Econometrics, Macmillan, second edition, 1985.

Lane, M.R., and Lane, S.A., Computer Education, 1984.

Ledin, G.,& Ledin, V., The Programmer's Book of Rules. Belmont, CA: Lifetime Learning Publications, 1979.

Mack, B. & Heath, P. (Eds.), Guide to Good Programming. New York: Halsted Press, 1980.

Mager, R. F., Preparing Instructional Objectives. Belmont, CA: Fearon, 1982.

Markle, S. M., Good Frames and Bad: A Grammar of Frame Writing, New York: John Wiley, 1989.

Mehrens, W.A. & Lehmann, I.J., Measurement and Evaluation in Education and Psychology, New York: Holt, Rienhart & Winston, 1983.

Merrill, M.D. & Tennyson, R. D., Teaching Concepts: An Instructional Design Guide, Englewood Cliffs, NJ: Educational Technology Publications, 1987.

Monica R. Brantley, Students Produce with Power Point: Using Multimedia in High School Geometry, 2001.

Naughton, Patrick and Schildt, Herbert., The Complete Reference Java 2, Third Edition, Tata McGraw-Hill Publishing Company Ltd., New Delhi, 2002.

Papert, S., Mind Storms, Children, Computer. Powerful Ideas, Harvester Press, United Kingdom, 1980.

Phalavonk, Utomporn, Achievement and Motivational Effects of Computer - Assisted Instruction for University Mathematics in Thailand, Ph.D thesis, University of New South Wales, Australia, 1991.

Pieme, T. E., Computer Assisted Learning and Evaluation in Medicine, *Journal of American Medical Association,* July 1988.

Plomp, T. and Moonen. J., Implementation of Computer in Education, International Journal of Educational Research, 1992.

Powels, Margaret, Women's Participation in Tertiary Education: A Review of Recent Australian Research: A Study Commissioned by the Commonwealth Tertiary Education Commission, Australia, 1986.

Pressman, R.S. Software Engineering: A Practitioners's Approach, New York: McGraw-Hill, 1992.

Riddle, W., & Wiledon, J., Tutorial on Software Design: Description and Analysis. Los Alamitos, CA: IEEE Computer Society Press, 1980.

Rinaldi, I.L., A Study of the Effects of Computer Assisted Instruction and Teacher Instruction of Achievement in Mathematics, Eastern Michigan University, 1997.

Ryan, M.G., The Effects of Computer Assisted Instruction on AT-RISK Technical College students, University of South Carolina, 1994.

Sadatman, Kamal Deen, The Effect of Computer Assisted Instruction on Algebraic Problem-solving Abilities of Community College Students, United States International University, 1995.

Sarasa, B., Effectiveness of Computer Assisted Instruction in the learning of Mathematics of Higher Secondary Girls - Unpublished Ph.D thesis - Mother Terasa Womens' University, Chennai,1992.

Saveiyan, A. and Venua, V., Higher Education and Computerisation, Progress Publications, Moscow, 1989.

Schwartz, Helen J., Geest, T.V.D. and Smit-Kreuzen, Marlies, Computers in Writing Instruction, *International Journal of Educational Research*, Volume 17, No. 1, 1992.

Selvam, M., Satisfaction Index, Tourism Industry in India.

Shiah, R., The effects of Computer Assisted Instruction on the Mathematical Problem - Solving of Students with Learning Disabilities, Purdue University, 1994.

Shneiderman, B., Software Psychology. Cambridge, MA: Winthrop Publishers, 1980.

Silbert, J., Carnine, D. and Stein, M., Direct Instruction Mathematics. Columbus, OH: Chas E. Merrill, 1981.

Srinivasa Raghavan, Micro Computers in Science and Language Teaching - A Booklet, Vivek Printers, Mysore, 1986.

Stern, N. B., Flowcharting: A Tool for Understanding Computer Logic. New York: John Wiley, 1985.

Stervart, James, Calculus-Fourth edition, Brooks/Cole Publishing company, ITP, 2001.

Tetlock, K.D., Implementing Computer Assisted Instruction in the Mathematics Classroom: Effect on Student Attitudes and the Teaching Process, The University of Manitoba (Canada), 1995.

Thomas, Robert M., Encyclopedia AUTOCAD Release 11, BPB Publications, New Delhi, 1992.

Tuckman, B.W., Conducting Educational Research, New York, Harcourt Brace Jovanovich, 1988.

Venkatasubramanian, K., A Case for Computerization, '*The Hindu*', February, 1992.

Walker, D.F. & Hess, R.D. Instructional Software: Principles and Perspectives for Design and Use. Belmont, CA: Wadsworth, 1984.

Wileman, R. E. Exercises in Visual Thinking, New York: Hastings House, 1980.

Williams, Clive and Tome, Pepe, Commonwealth Tertiary Education Commission, Australia, 1983.